CW00537658

A
BEGINNER'S
ILLUSTRATED
HANDBOOK

Swords of Japan

Yasuko Kubo

Translated by
Paul Martin

**TOKYO
BIJUTSU**

Introduction

The Japanese sword is a cultural symbol of Japan, and known throughout the world. Even though they are fundamentally weapons, the high level of skills involved to produce such a beautiful and effective sword raises their value greatly, making them sacred objects and symbols of authority.

About a thousand years have passed since the birth of the Japanese sword. During this long history the shape has changed many times according to era of manufacture, but the light of Japanese swords still shines brightly in the hearts of the Japanese people today.

Yasuko Kubo
September 2016

The Allure of Japanese Swords

Many people probably appreciate the elegant curve of Japanese swords. The way in which a Japanese sword is manufactured reflects the period in which it was made. Additionally, by examining the finely polished surface steel and various patterns of the hardened edge (hamon), one can determine the province, school and even maker.

The blades protective mountings are made by several different specialist craftsmen all using traditional techniques. Japanese swords are unique to Japanese culture, and are unparalleled in the world.

A very elegantly curved blade with a carving of a Sanko-tsuki-ken*

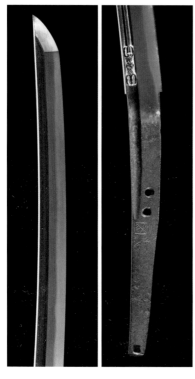

National Treasure **Tachi**

Mei: **Kuniyuki** (Rai) 銘:国行 (来)

Mid-Kamakura period 13th C.
Nagasa: 76.6 cm Yamashiro Province (Kyoto).

Kuniyuki is said to be the founder of the Rai school in Yamashiro province. The deepest part of the curvature is in the center of the blade. This blade was an heirloom of the Matsudaira family of Akashi, Harima province (Hyogo prefecture).

*p.48

An austere, unique masterpiece from among the Yamato school blades

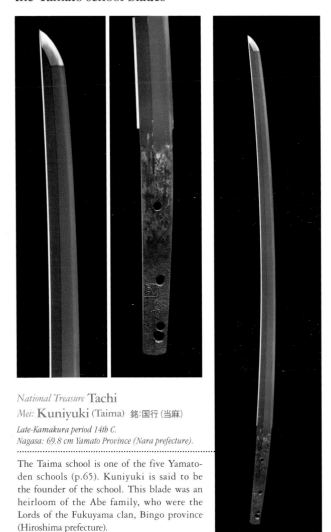

National Treasure Tachi
Mei: **Kuniyuki** (Taima) 銘:国行 (当麻)

Late-Kamakura period 14th C.
Nagasa: 69.8 cm Yamato Province (Nara prefecture).

The Taima school is one of the five Yamato-den schools (p.65). Kuniyuki is said to be the founder of the school. This blade was an heirloom of the Abe family, who were the Lords of the Fukuyama clan, Bingo province (Hiroshima prefecture).

This sword belonged to Emperor Go-mizuno. It is a sword of excellent quality with that is very clear in the ji and ha

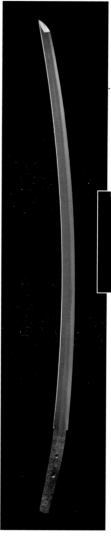

National Treasure Tachi
Mei: Nobuyoshi (Ryumon)
銘:延吉 (龍門)

Late-Kamakura period 14th C.
Nagasa: 73.4 cm Yamato Province
(Nara prefecture).

Nobuyoshi was a smith of the Senjuin school (p.65), and resided at Ryumon in Yoshino, Yamato province. He worked in two styles, Yamato-den and Bizen-den. This blade is in the Bizen style of workmanship.

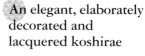

An elegant, elaborately decorated and lacquered koshirae

Kin-nashiji lacquer saya with interspersed chrysanthemum mon

Tachi koshirae of the Nobuyoshi blade (L.)
Early-Edo period 17th C.

The saya has fine mother-of-pearl chrysanthemum mon inlaid on a nashiji lacquer ground.

The pride of Bizen can be felt in this powerful shape

Important Cultural Property

Tachi

Mei: **Masatsune** 銘:正恒

Early-Kamakura period 12th C.
Nagasa: 78.4 cm Bizen Province
(Okayama prefecture).

This blade was made by Masatsune of the Ko-Bizen school. His extant works date from the late Heian period through to the Kamakura period. This blade is one of those signed works. It is generally a very healthy blade. It was an heirloom of the Ogasawara family of the Kokura clan of Buzen province (Fukuoka prefecture).

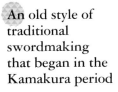

An old style of traditional swordmaking that began in the Kamakura period

The black lacquered tachi koshirae

Tachi koshirae of the Masatsune blade (L.)
Nanbokucho period 14th C.

The slender, flat saya is wrapped in leather and lacquered to give it strength.

1

This blade displays typical Ko-Bizen characteristics. It is a graceful blade of the highest quality

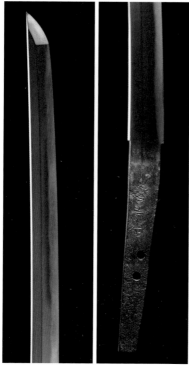

Important Cultural Property Tachi
Mei: Nobufusa Saku 銘:信房作

Late-Heian, early-Kamakura period 12th C.
Nagasa: 76.2 cm Bizen Province (Okayama prefecture).

This blade is by Nobufusa of the Ko-Bizen school. An heirloom of the Ikeda family of Inaba province (Tottori prefecture), it was presented to them by the eighth Tokugawa shogun, Yoshimune.

Master smith Nagamitsu. A high level of skill is displayed along the whole length of the blade

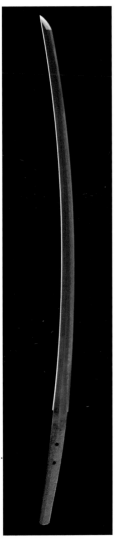

National Treasure Tachi
Mei: **Kumano Sansho Gongen Nagamitsu** 銘:熊野三所権現長光

Mid to late-Kamakura period 13th-14th C.
Nagasa: 74.8 cm Bizen Province (Okayama prefecture).

Nagamitsu was from the Osafune school in Bizen province. The ubu-nakago (original condition from time of manufacture) is inscribed *Kumano Sansho Gongen Nagamitsu*. The Kuki family of Kumano were very powerful. They presented this sword to the Tokugawa shogunal family.

Meibutsu: Nami Oyogi Kanemitsu
A blade with a dignified shape and a carving of a dragon

Important Art Object **Katana**
*Kinzogan-mei: Nami oyoki Matsudai no ken Kanemitsu nari Hashiba Okayama Chunagon Hide ☐ Shoji Kore

金象嵌銘:波およき末代劔兼光也
　　　　羽柴岡山中納言秀□所持之

Nanbokucho period 14th C.
Nagasa: 64.8 cm Bizen Province
(Okayama prefecture).

Kanemitsu was a smith from the Osafune school in Bizen province who worked in the Nanbokucho period (14th C.). According to an old legend, a person who was cut with the blade managed to swim to the other shore before falling into two parts. The blade was owned by Chunagon* Hideaki, who was the adopted son of Kobayakawa Takakage. This blade was an heirloom of the Yanagawa, Tachibana family of Chikugo province (Fukuoka prefecture).

*kinzogan is when a gold inlaid inscription is used to authenticate an unsigned blade.
*a counsellor of the second rank to the imperial court.

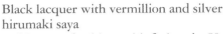 A beautiful and refined color scheme

Black lacquer with vermillion and silver hirumaki saya
Uchi-gatana koshirae with fittings by Yasuchika
Mid-Edo period 17th C.

The saya has a black lacquered ray-skin ground wrapped alternately in strips of vermillion and silver. This was a sword of Satsuma (Kagoshima prefecture) Kuroda Kiyotaka.

The menuki are images of galloping horses.

An elegant Chinese tale themed tsuba by Yasuchika

Chokaro sukashi tsuba *Mei:* Yasuchika 銘:安親

This tsuba is by Tsuchiya Yasuchika, a prominent fittings maker of the mid-Edo period. He was born in Tsuruoka, Dewa province (Yamagata prefecture), but moved to Kanda in Edo (Tokyo). He was very skilled and developed his own unique style.

Chokaro was a Chinese sage (and one of the eight immortals). He is seen riding a white mule. One of the old tales of Chokaro says that when he wanted to rest, he would fold his mule up like a sheet of paper. Then, when he wanted to ride it again he sprinkled water on it from his gourd, and it turned back into a mule.

An important example of a Higo koshirae with beautiful Kuyo-mon fittings

Higo uchi-gatana koshirae with an aizame togidashi saya and Kuyo-mon fittings

Late-Edo period 19th C.

....

The fittings are by Kobayashi Takatada of Higo province (Kumamoto prefecture). The theme is the Hosokawa clan crest (Kuyo-mon). Kobayashi was retained by the Hosokawa clan. The saya is wrapped in Aizame (a type of shark-skin), lacquered black, and then polished to reveal the skin pattern.

A rare stork's leg skin saya. This koshirae was an heirloom of the Tokugawa shogunal family

Stork's leg skin wrapped saya with Aoi-mon denchu-kojiri saya uchi-gatana koshirae

Late-Edo period 19th C.

....

The kojiri is known as a denchu-kojiri. The kojiri is wider than the koi-guchi, and is angular with one side longer than the other. A very rare example, the koshirae is wrapped in the skin of stork's legs, and has applied black lacquer Aoi-mon. This koshirae was given by the Tokugawa shogunal family to Yamaoka Tesshu, and was later passed to Iwakura Tomomi.

This rather flamboyant work is by Kiyotsuna, the founder of the Nio school

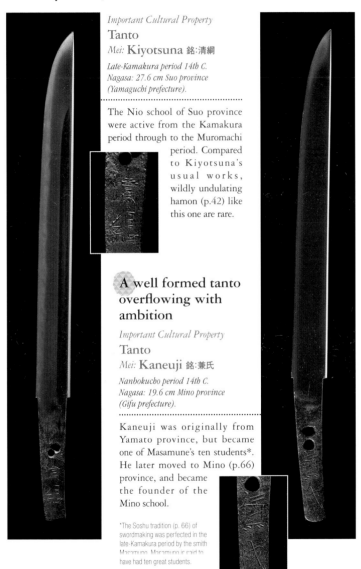

Important Cultural Property

Tanto

Mei: **Kiyotsuna** 銘:清綱

Late-Kamakura period 14th C.
Nagasa: 27.6 cm Suo province
(Yamaguchi prefecture).

The Nio school of Suo province were active from the Kamakura period through to the Muromachi period. Compared to Kiyotsuna's usual works, wildly undulating hamon (p.42) like this one are rare.

A well formed tanto overflowing with ambition

Important Cultural Property

Tanto

Mei: **Kaneuji** 銘:兼氏

Nanbokucho period 14th C.
Nagasa: 19.6 cm Mino province
(Gifu prefecture).

Kaneuji was originally from Yamato province, but became one of Masamune's ten students*. He later moved to Mino (p.66) province, and became the founder of the Mino school.

*The Soshu tradition (p. 66) of swordmaking was perfected in the late-Kamakura period by the smith Masamune. Masamune is said to have had ten great students.

A flamboyant koshirae with gold-colored sacred beasts

A hardwood koshi-gatana koshirae with sacred beasts design saya

Edo period 17th-19th C.

....

Many types of lacquer all on one saya

A chisa-gatana koshirae with patchwork lacquer saya and a plain wooden tsuka

Edo period 17th-19th C.

....

Both of these tanto koshirae are made from rare woods. The one on the left is a rather bright, flamboyant koshirae with mythical sacred beasts in gold. The sacred beasts are dragons (kozuka, kogai and fuchi), phoenixes (saya), kirin (menuki), and a kind of mythical tortoise called reiki (kurikata and kojiri). The koshirae on the right has a patchwork display of various types of lacquer techniques.

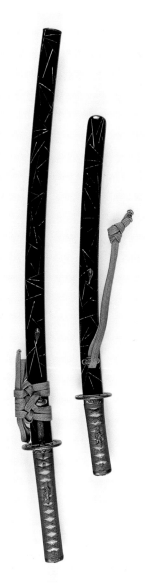

🌑 An auspicious hiwari* design raden daisho koshirae

Daisho koshirae with a
black lacquered
and inlaid mother of pearl
hiwari design saya

Late-Edo period 19th C.

A daisho is a formalised matching
pair of long (uchi-gatana) and short
(wakizashi) swords. The wearing of
daisho was first established in the
late-Muromachi period. In the Edo
period, daisho with black lacquer saya
had become official formal wear for
attendance at the castle. The hiwari
design represents the cracking of ice
underfoot when stepping outside to
observe the sunrise on the morning
of the first day of the new year. The
design is auspicious as it captures
the feeling of the reflection of the
brightness of the first sunrise.

*Hiwari (cracked ice)

Sparrows in the sea with clams design daisho tsuba (front)

Sparrows in the sea with clams design daisho tsuba (back)

Sparrow Themed Fittings

Parts of the Koshirae

The fittings from the daisho koshirae on the previous page have a sparrow theme design. The maker has made full use of a wide variety of carefully chosen colored metals. The tsuba has a sparrows in the sea with clams design depicting a beach in late-autumn with excited sparrows that resemble clams. The theme comes from an old tale of sparrows becoming clams when they go into the sea. If you look closely at the back of the clam you can see a sparrow's face.

Kozuka and kogai from the uchi-gatana koshirae

Genpei Battle Scene Mi-tokoro-mono
Kozuka mei: Goto Eijo (kao)
Kogai: Kinzogan-mei Goto Eijo (kao)
Menuki: Unsigned attributed to Goto Eijo

Momoyama period 17th C.

The three fittings of a kozuka, kogai and set of menuki (p.106) are collectively referred to as mi-tokoro-mono when they are a matching set. This set depicts various scenes of the battles between the Taira and Minamoto clans. The maker is the sixth generation head of the Iebori Goto family. He is well known for making fittings with battle scenes like this set. They are filled with skillful depictions of samurai warriors in armor. Extant signed works by Eijo are extremely rare.

Kogai

Kozuka

Menuki

Making the Blade ···· 67

Polishing the Blade ···· 83

Sword Fittings and Mountings ···· 93

APPENDICES ···· 109

Japanese Sword Basics

*All the parts of a Japanese sword are named using
special terminology. Also, the various types
of blades are classified using modern definitions.
In this next section,
we will look at the changes in Japanese swords
through the different historical periods.*

Terminology for the Different Parts of a Japanese Sword

This diagram explains the names of the different parts of the blade. This unique set of terms are frequently used when explaining about Japanese swords.

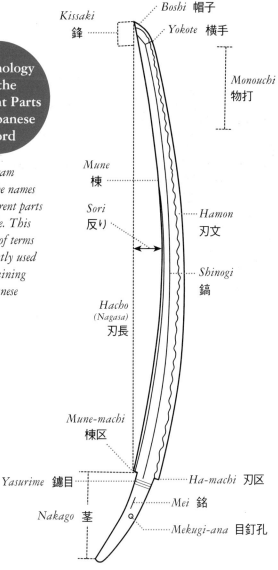

Boshi 帽子

Kissaki 鋒

Yokote 横手

Monouchi 物打

Mune 棟

Sori 反り

Hamon 刃文

Shinogi 鎬

Hacho (Nagasa) 刃長

Mune-machi 棟区

Yasurime 鑢目

Ha-machi 刃区

Nakago 茎

Mei 銘

Mekugi-ana 目釘孔

A General Overview of Japanese Swords

C urrently, when we hear the term 'Japanese sword', the image of a curved tachi comes to mind. This shape of sword first appeared from the mid-Heian period onwards. Before that time straight swords known as chokuto were used. Straight swords are more suitable for thrusting rather than slashing. From these swords evolved the curved tachi that was suitable for slashing.

The largest factor in the change from the straight sword to the curved tachi is the change in combat styles. Unlike the era of the straight sword, from the late-Heian period the curved sword and bow and arrow proved useful weapons for cavalry warfare. Additionally, improvements were made from battle experience, and combat effeciancy was researched and improved.

During the late-Heian and early-Kamakura periods five main centers of manufacturing arose as the foundation of all sword-making across the country. The provinces were Yamato, Yamashiro, Bizen, Sagami and later Mino. From the Meiji period onwards, they were referred to as the Gokaden (p.64).

Swords made from the start of the Edo period are referred to as Shinto (new swords). At this time, a new tradition arose mixing old traditions with new techniques giving rise to makers across the country. Those techniques are the basis for swords made today in Japan.

A Chart of Japanese Historical Periods

The style of Japanese swords change according to the various eras.

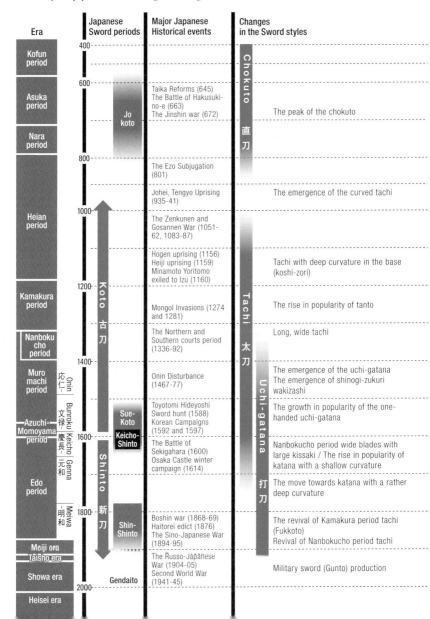

Era	Japanese Sword periods	Major Japanese Historical events	Changes in the Sword styles
Kofun period	400		**Chokuto 直刀** — The peak of the chokuto
Asuka period	600 / Jo koto	Taika Reforms (645) / The Battle of Hakusuki-no-e (663) / The Jinshin war (672)	
Nara period	800		
Heian period		The Ezo Subjugation (801)	
		Johei, Tengyo Uprising (935-41)	The emergence of the curved tachi
	1000	The Zenkunen and Gosannen War (1051-62, 1083-87)	
		Hogen uprising (1156) / Heiji uprising (1159) / Minamoto Yoritomo exiled to Izu (1160)	Tachi with deep curvature in the base (koshi-zori)
Kamakura period	1200 / Koto 古刀	Mongol Invasions (1274 and 1281)	**Tachi 太刀** — The rise in popularity of tanto
Nanboku cho period		The Northern and Southern courts period (1336-92)	Long, wide tachi
Muro machi period	1400 / Onin 応仁	Onin Disturbance (1467-77)	The emergence of the uchi-gatana / The emergence of shinogi-zukuri wakizashi
Azuchi-Momoyama period	Bunroku 文禄 / Keicho 慶長 / Sue-Koto / Keicho-Shinto	Toyotomi Hideyoshi Sword hunt (1588) / Korean Campaigns (1592 and 1597)	**Uchi-gatana** — The growth in popularity of the one-handed uchi-gatana
	Genna 元和 / Shinto 新刀	The Battle of Sekigahara (1600) / Osaka Castle winter campaign (1614)	Nanbokucho period wide blades with large kissaki / The rise in popularity of katana with a shallow curvature
Edo period	1600		The move towards katana with a rather deep curvature
	1800 / Meiwa 明和 / 新刀 / Shin-Shinto	Boshin war (1868-69) / Haitorei edict (1876) / The Sino-Japanese War (1894-95)	**打刀** — The revival of Kamakura period tachi (Fukkoto) / Revival of Nanbokucho period tachi
Meiji era / **Taisho era**		The Russo-Japanese War (1904-05) / Second World War (1941-45)	Military sword (Gunto) production
Showa era	Gendaito		
Heisei era	2000		

There are various sizes and shapes of Japanese swords. They have been broken down here into eight broad categories.

Chokuto
(straight swords)
● 直刀

Chokuto are swords with little or no curvature. However, swords made between the Kofun and Nara periods have gained a slight uchi-zori (inward curvature). The shinogi (ridgeline) does not appear on hira-zukuri blades, and with kiriha-zukuri blades the shinogi is closer to the cutting edge. Modern made chokuto can still be seen today.

A haniwa (clay figure), holding the tsuka (handle) of his chokuto in his right hand.

Tachi

 太刀

Tachi are usually displayed
in museums and art galleries
with the cutting edge facing
downwards. This is because,
from the late-Heian period
(12th C.) through to the early-
Muromachi period (14th C.)
swords were worn suspended
from the belt with the cutting
edge facing downwards.
They have a deep curvature
and have a cutting edge of
about 70 cm to 80 cm (2.3 to
2.6 shaku) in length. Tachi
were still manufactured in
the Shinto (Keicho era 1596
-1614), Bakumatsu, and Shin-
shinto sword making eras.

Katana

● 刀

The tachi was modified into the katana around the mid-Muromachi period (late 15th C.), and were used right through to the mid 19th C. They have a cutting edge of 60.6cm (2 shaku) or over. However, they are generally shorter than tachi. As opposed to the tachi, they are worn thrust through the sash with the cutting edge uppermost. Originally, shortened tachi were called katana, and worn cutting edge uppermost thrust through the sash.

Also referred to as uchi-gatana.

26

Wakizashi
● 脇指

Wakizashi are short swords with a cutting edge of longer than 30.3cm (1 shaku), and under 60.6cm (2 shaku). Just like katana, they are worn thrust through the sash. Ko-wakizashi are short wakizashi with a cutting edge of approximately 36~40cm (1.2 to 1.3 shaku) in length. In the Momoyama and Edo periods, a matching pair of swords called a daisho were worn.

Only wakizashi were allowed to be worn inside the castle.

Tanto (dagger)
● 短刀

Tanto are daggers with a cutting edge of less than 30.3cm (1 shaku) in length, and are also called koshi-gatana. They are usually hira-zukuri in construction.

Futokoro-gatana
● 懐刀

A small dagger kept close to the body for self defence. Also known as a *kaiken tanto*. The meaning has been adapted to mean a secret kept amongst a circle of colleagues.

Ken
● 剣

A ken is a straight dagger with a cutting edge on both sides. In the Shinto period of sword making, ken with a yokote (dividing line at the kissaki) can be seen.

Naginata
● 薙刀

A naginata has a long nakago and is usually mounted as a pole arm. They are curved in the upper section of the blade. Some have a cutting edge on both sides of the blade in the tip area.

SWORD RELATED
PHRASES

Tachi-Ojo
● 立ち往生

Originally the meaning was to die in a standing position. Nowadays, it means to be caught between a rock and a hard place. Benkei was hit by countless arrows at the battle of Koromo river and is said to have died standing holding his naginata. This story is called *Benkei no Tachi-ojo.*

Yari
● 槍

A yari is a spear with a ken shaped blade on the end of a long pole. The shapes and sizes of blades and poles change according to period and usage. The blade types include ryo-shinogi, hira-sankaku, sasaho, jumonji, katakama. They are broadly split into two types, straight yari and jumonji (ones with a blade coming out of each side at the bottom).

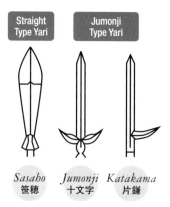

Straight Type Yari

Jumonji Type Yari

Sasaho
笹穂

Jumonji
十文字

Katakama
片鎌

30

Important Points of Sword Manufacture

*With each advancing era,
the swordsmiths manufacturing techniques
and methods changed.
In this section, we look at the important points of
manufacture and the different parts
of the sword.*

Tsukuri-komi
(construction types)
● 造込み

Tsukuri-komi is the Japanese word used to describe the type of blade construction. For example, hira-zukuri, kiriha-zukuri, shinogi-zukuri, and so forth.

Hira-zukuri
● 平造

Cross-sectional diagram

A blade construction without a shinogi. Tanto and wakizashi are mostly seen in this type of construction.

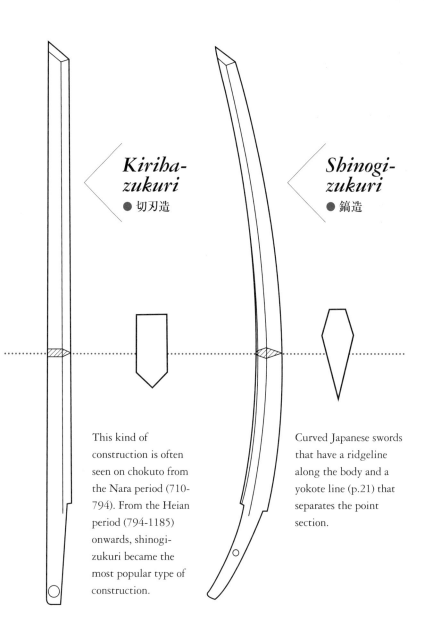

Kiriha-zukuri
● 切刃造

This kind of construction is often seen on chokuto from the Nara period (710-794). From the Heian period (794-1185) onwards, shinogi-zukuri became the most popular type of construction.

Shinogi-zukuri
● 鎬造

Curved Japanese swords that have a ridgeline along the body and a yokote line (p.21) that separates the point section.

Mune
● 棟

Nakago
● 茎

Nakago-jiri

● 茎尻

The mune, nakago and nakago-jiri all differ in shape according to period and schools of manufacture. They are an important appraisal point.

Mune ● 棟

The mune is the spine of the blade on the opposite side to the cutting edge. There are three main types of mune, iori-mune, mitsu-mune and maru-mune. The most common is iori-mune. However, depending on sword-making school mitsu-mune and maru-mune can be seen too.

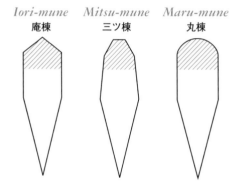

| *Iori-mune* | *Mitsu-mune* | *Maru-mune* |
| 庵棟 | 三ツ棟 | 丸棟 |

High or Low Shinogi

As can be seen in the cross-sectional diagrams below, when the blade is wide at the shinogi, it is said to have a high shinogi, and when the blade is slender at the shinogi, it is called a low shinogi. High or low shinogi is one of the terms used when describing a blade.

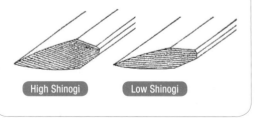

High Shinogi   Low Shinogi

Nakago ● 茎

The nakago is the section of the blade to which the handle is attached. The way in which the nakago and the nakago-jiri are finished varies according to school and makers.

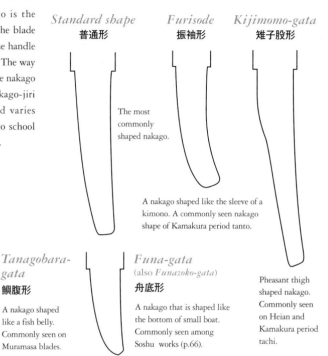

Standard shape
普通形

The most commonly shaped nakago.

Furisode
振袖形

A nakago shaped like the sleeve of a kimono. A commonly seen nakago shape of Kamakura period tanto.

Kijimomo-gata
雉子股形

Pheasant thigh shaped nakago. Commonly seen on Heian and Kamakura period tachi.

Tanagobara-gata
鱮腹形

A nakago shaped like a fish belly. Commonly seen on Muramasa blades.

Funa-gata
(also *Funazoko-gata*)
舟底形

A nakago that is shaped like the bottom of small boat. Commonly seen among Soshu works (p.66).

Nakago-jiri ● 茎尻

The very end of the nakago is called the nakago-jiri. Kuri-jiri was the most common shape during the Koto and Shinto periods of sword manufacture, but all types can be seen.

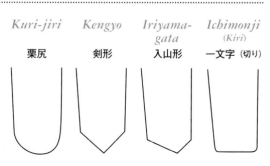

Kuri-jiri
栗尻

Kengyo
剣形

Iriyama-gata
入山形

Ichimonji
(*Kiri*)
一文字 (切り)

Kitae
(forging)

● 鍛え

In order to meet the three requirements of 'not bending, not breaking and cutting well' a core of softer, lower carbon steel is wrapped in a jacket of higher carbon hard steel and forged into a blade. The higher carbon jacket steel is folded between 8-15 times. Kitae is a word used to describe the forge-folding process, that produces a wood-grain-like pattern called hada that is visible on the steel surface.

Shingane ● 心鉄
(low-carbon softer steel)

Soft iron

Cross-sectional diagram of blade

Kawagane ● 皮鉄
(higher-carbon hard steel)

Hard iron

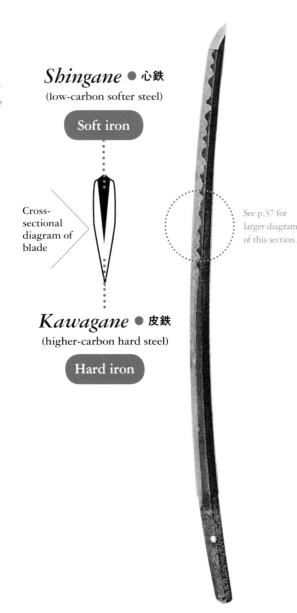

See p.37 for larger diagrams of this section.

The Four Main Types of Forging Patterns

Itame-hada ● 板目肌

This is the most commonly seen type of hada pattern. Especially large sized pattern is called o-itame. This kind of hada pattern can be see among the Soshu-den works of the famous smith Masamune, and the works of the smiths of Hoki province (Tottori and Shimane prefectures). A tightly forged itame or ko-itame hada is commonly seen on the works of Kamakura period Yamashiro (Kyoto) smiths. Particularly fine, well-forged works are referred to as Nashiji-hada (Japanese pear skin).

Mokume-hada ● 杢目肌

Mokume-hada appears like the rings of a tree and is often mixed with itame-hada. Works with particularly prominent mokume-hada includes the Aoe school of Bitchu province (West Okayama prefecture). This school's hada is said to resemble the texture of chirimen silk crepe, so it is referred to as chirimen-hada.

Masame-hada ● 柾目肌

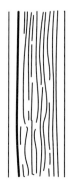

Masame-hada is similar to a straight wood grain pattern. It is seen among the works of the Yamato schools (p.65) from the mid-Heian period onwards, particularly in the blades of the Hosho school and their disciples.

Ayasugi-hada ● 綾杉肌

Ayasugi is a type of hada with large undulations like a row of cryptomeria trees. It is associated with the Gassan school of Mutsu province (Iwate prefecture) and is often called Gassan-hada, but it can also be seen in the works of the Naminohira school of Satsuma province (Kagoshima prefecture).

Nie and *Nioi*

● 沸と匂

At the time of yaki-ire (quenching) a line is created separating the hard cutting edge, and the softer body of the blade. In this border between the hamon and the ji, tiny crystal formations called nie and nioi appear.

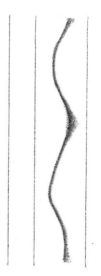

Nie are larger crystals that are individually visible to the naked eye, as opposed to nioi crystals that appear misty and can only be seen individually under a microscope. Nie sparkle like stars in the night sky, while nioi resembles the glowing mistiness of the milky way.

Nioi
匂

SWORD RELATED PHRASES

Tsuke-yakiba
● 付け焼き刃

Tsuke-yakiba means either a blade that has not been heat treated and cannot hold a cutting edge, or a sword that has a hamon-like pattern applied, but is blunt. As they are unusable, the phrase has come to mean someone who does not possess enough knowledge or deep enough skills.

39

Activities Within the *Ha*

● 刃中の働き

Various activities appear in the hardened section of the blade due to the interaction of crystaline formations with the structure of the surface steel.

Activities in the Ji and the Ha

Ashi
● 足

Saka-ashi
● 逆足

Yo
● 葉

Depending on the structure of the hamon, various activities appear: ashi, saka-ashi, yo, sunagashi, kinsuji, uchinoke and so forth. Nie does not only appear in the ha, it can also be present in the body of the blade. This is referred to as ji-nie.

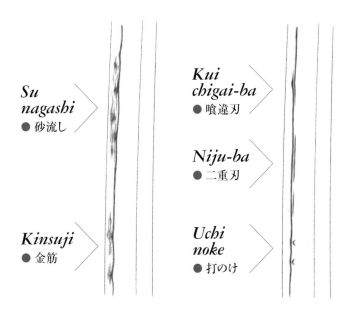

Su nagashi
● 砂流し

Kui chigai-ba
● 喰違刃

Niju-ba
● 二重刃

Kinsuji
● 金筋

Uchi noke
● 打のけ

Works with prevalent nie in the ha are referred to as nie-deki. The works of Masamune of the Soshu school (p.66) are the prime example of nie-deki works, and would also have kinsuji and sunagashi. The representative schools for nioi-deki works are the Bizen works from the mid-Kamakura period onwards and the Nanbokucho works of the Aoe school. Ashi and yo are often seen in the ha. Also, among the masame works of the Yamato school (p.65), it is common to see activities such as kuichigai-ba, niju-ba and uchinoke.

Hamon
● 刃文

The pattern of the hamon is created by the application of clay and yaki-ire process. After the blade has had a rough finishing, a thin layer of clay is painted along the cutting edge, and a thicker layer of clay is applied to the back of the blade (p.78). Depending on the method in which the clay is applied effects the outcome of the pattern of the hamon, If the clay is applied in a straight line, the hamon will be suguha. If it is applied in an irregular manner, it will become midare. The beauty of the hamon is another aspect of Japanese swords that is appreciated by enthusiasts.

Types of Hamon

There are various types of hamon. Even suguha comes in different types depending on width: hoso-suguha, chu-suguha, hiro-suguha, and so forth. Among the undulating types there are, ko-midare, choji, gunome, notare, toran-ba, hitatsura, etc. They come in all manner of styles.

 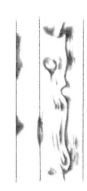

Toran-ba
● 濤乱刃

Hitatsura
● 皆焼

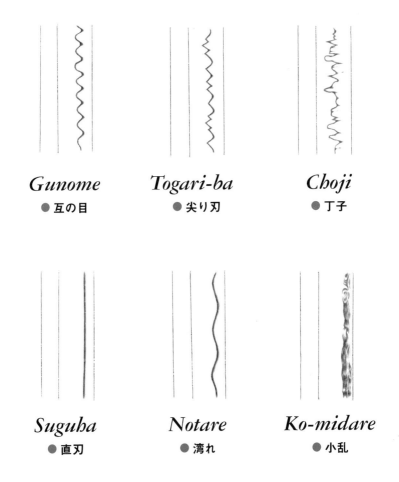

Gunome
● 互の目

Togari-ba
● 尖り刃

Choji
● 丁子

Suguha
● 直刃

Notare
● 湾れ

Ko-midare
● 小乱

Boshi
● 帽子

The point section of the blade is called the kissaki. The hamon in this section of the blade is referred to as the boshi. Kissaki sizes, shapes and boshi reflect various periods of workmanship and the characteristics of individual swordsmiths. It is a very important point in sword appraisal.

Types of Boshi

There are various terms for the shapes and condition of boshi, such as o-maru, ko-maru, midare-komi, yakizume, ichi-mai, and so forth.

O-maru
● 大丸

Ko-maru
● 小丸

44

Ichi-mai
● 一枚

Yakizume
(with *hakikake*)

● 焼詰め（掃きかける）

Midare-komi
● 乱れ込み

Saki-togaru
(pointed)

● 先尖る

Short Kaeri
● 返り浅い

Long Kaeri
● 返り深い

Nakago Yasurime
(filemarks)
● 茎の鑢目

It is thought that the yasurime (filemarks) on the nakago (tang) were originally help to secure the tsuka. There are various types of yasurime that display the characteristics of various smiths, and schools.

Types of Yasurime

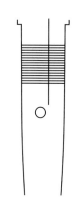

Kiri (Horizontal)
切 （横）

Horizontal filemarks. The most common type of filemarks.

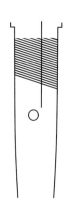

Katte-sagari
勝手下り

Katte means 'right-hand'. Katte-sagari means filemarks that slope down to the right. This is the second most common type of filemark after kiri.

SWORD RELATED PHRASES
Aizuchi wo Utsu
● 相鎚を打つ

When the swordsmith is forging swords he has hammer men opposite him to hammer with him. This saying means to be in accord with someone.

46

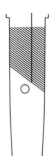

Sujikai
筋違

Filemarks that slope down at a steeper angle than katte-sagari. If they slope down to the left, they are called gyaku-sujikai.

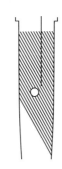

O-sujikai
大筋違

Filemarks that are steeper than sujikai. Seen on the works of the Koto period Aoe, and Sa schools.

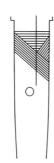

Kesho-yasuri
化粧鑢

An elaborate type of filemarks used by various smiths. Seen on the Shinto blades from the Edo period onwards.

Sensuki
鏟鋤

A sen is a type of metal draw-knife or plane. These type of tool markings are often found on the nakago of jokoto blades and naginata.

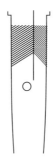

Taka-no-ha
鷹羽

Filemarks that resemble a hawk's feather. Also called shida.

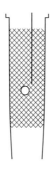

Higaki
檜垣

A series of criss-crossing diagonal lines resulting is a diamond shaped pattern. Seen on the works of the Yamato, Mino, and the Satsuma Naminohira schools.

Horimono
(blade carvings)
● 刀身彫刻

Horimono are carvings made into the surface of the blade. They can be seen to have been carved in blades since the Heian period. They can be practical, but are also carved for religious and decorative reasons. They change in accordance with the styles and beliefs of various periods.

Fudo Myo-o ● 不動明王

Kurikara ● 倶利伽羅

Sanko-tsuki-ken ● 三鈷付剣

Among the blades of the Koto period of sword manufacture (~1600), many of the carvings display religious meaning: Bonji (sanskrit), Su-ken, Fudo Myo-o, Kurikara, Sanko-tsuki-ken, Goma-bashi, Hachiman-daibosatsu, Namu-myoho-renge-kyo, and Sanjuban-shin.

In the Shinto period of swordmaking (1600~), the carvings become more decorative with depictions of cranes and turtles, ascending and descending dragons, shochikubai (pine, bamboo and plum), and the deity of wealth, Daikoku.

48

The Evolution of the Shape of the Japanese Sword

*Straight swords were originally imported from the continent
into Japan, but they were soon shaped by warfare
until they obtained their unique Japanese sword shape.
The changes in shape can be seen in accordance
with the various historical eras.
Next, we will look at the various characteristics
of the different eras.*

Changes in the Shape of Japanese Swords According to Era

1
Before the Nara period.

2
Late-Heian through early-Kamakura periods (late 12th to early 13th C.)

3
Mid-Kamakura period (13th C.)

4
Late-Kamakura period (late 13th to early 14th C.)

5
Nanbokucho period (14th C.)

Mostly hira-zukuri and kiriha-zukuri chokuto blades (without curvature).

Shinogi-zukuri blades appear with curvature. The center of curvature is deepest in the base of the blade (koshi-zori).

This era was the peak of the warrior class. Many fine robust tachi were produced.

The kissaki becomes extended, and slight curvature appears the upper part of the blade. Funbari (p.53) appears less prominent.

Blades become wide, large sized tachi with o-kissaki. No-dachi also appear in this period.

50

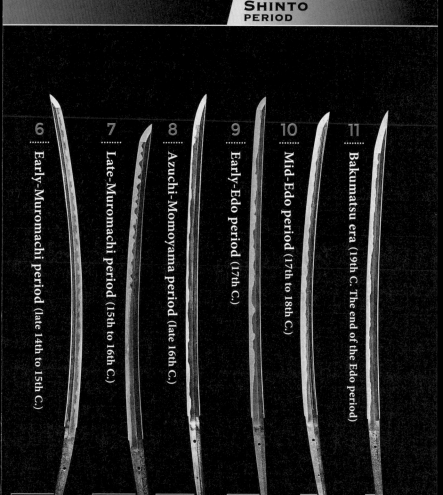

6 Early-Muromachi period (late 14th to 15th C.)

7 Late-Muromachi period (15th to 16th C.)

8 Azuchi-Momoyama period (late 16th C.)

9 Early-Edo period (17th C.)

10 Mid-Edo period (17th to 18th C.)

11 Bakumatsu era (19th C. The end of the Edo period)

Blades are similar in shape to that of the Kamakura period, except that they now also have curvature in the upper part of the blade (saki-zori).

The combat style changes to mass infantry warfare, and many uchi-gatana are produced.

Swords are produced in the same shape as Nanbokucho period blades, but in their shortened form.

The curvature becomes very shallow, and the blade narrows noticeably. This shape is called Kanbun-shinto.

Compared to Kanbun-shinto blades, swords of this era become deeper in curvature.

Many blades are recreated in the shapes of blades from the Kamakura and Nanbokucho periods.

JOKOTO PERIOD

1 Before the Nara Period

Jokoto blades are mostly hira-zukuri and kiriha-zukuri chokuto (blades without curvature). It is thought that the curve was introduced into the blade in the mid-Heian period around the mid-10th century. This was around the time of the uprisings by Taira Masakado and Fujiwara Sumitomo (Johei, Tengyo Uprisings). Before this time, blades are referred to as jokoto. Straight blades were originally imported from the continent. Many of the reference blades of this era were excavated from Kofun period tombs, or are in the collection of the Nara period Imperial repository, the Shoso-in, in Nara.

Shotoku Taishi wearing a chokuto in a black lacquered saya koshirae.

2 Late-Heian Through Early-Kamakura Periods
(late 12th to early 13th C.)

From the late Heian period we see the standard tachi shape appear. In other words, curved blades of shinogi-zukuri (ridgeline) construction.

They are generally slender, The base is comparatively wider than in the upper part of the blade, and they have a small point section. They have strong funbari.* The deepest part of the curvature is centered between the handle and base. This shape is called koshi-zori. From midway towards the point the blade becomes rather straight. They usually have a cutting edge length of around 75.8-78.8 cm (2.5 to 2.6 shaku) in length.

*Funbari means to fan out, or get wider towards the machi.

3 Mid-Kamakura Period
(13th C.)

The warrior class reached the peak of their power during the mid-Kamakura period. The blades kasane become thick, with a rich hira-niku. Compared to the previous period, the mihaba becomes wide and they have a magnificent tachi shape. The moto-haba and the saki-haba are of about even width. The blade is still koshi-zori, but the center of the curvature has moved a bit further along the blade. The kissaki is chu-kissaki, or sometimes a compact ikubi-kissaki type.

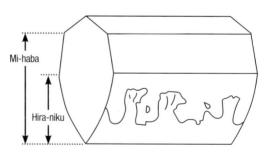

Mi-haba

Hira-niku

The kasane is thick, and the hira-niku is rich.

4 Late-Kamakura Period
(late 13th to early 14th C.)

The hira-niku of the tachi at the end of the Kamakura period are comparatively thin compared to tachi of the preceding period. Funbari appears less prominent. They no longer have ikubi-kissaki, but tend to have chu-kissaki or slightly extended chu-kissaki. In addition, they are quite slender and are similar in appearance to the shapes to the late Heian, and early Kamakura tachi. However, the upper part of the blade is no longer straight. It now has curvature.

SWORD RELATED
PHRASES

Tachi-uchi
● 太刀打ち

The original meaning was to 'fight with tachi', but nowadays the meaning has changed to 'compete with a rival'.

55

5 Nanbokucho Period (14th C.)

Blades become wide, large sized tachi with o-kissaki. Many extra long blades of 90.9cm (3 shaku) were made in this period. Large sized tanto were also produced. Among the tachi, some were worn over the back. These types of blade are called no-dachi and o-dachi. However, they were rather thin in construction, and many had bo-hi (grooves carved into the blade) to decrease the weight. Many tachi from this period were shortened (o-suriage) in later periods (mainly in the Tensho and Keicho eras). Consequently, many extant blades from the Nanbokucho period are unsigned.

A horse mounted warrior with an o-dachi resting on his shoulder, and a tachi with a saya wrapped in tiger skin at his hip.

6 Early-Muromachi Period
(late 14th to 15th C.)

Blades of the early-Muromachi period are similar in style to that of the Kamakura period. Unlike the blades of the previous Nanbokucho period, they are no longer over-sized with an o-kissaki. They are around 72.7cm-75.7cm (2.4 to 2.5 shaku) in length, rather slender, with funbari, a deep curvature, and a medium-sized point section. At first glance they resemble Kamakura period blades, but the kasane is thick, and there is a slight curvature in the upper-part of the blade (saki-zori).

SWORD RELATED
PHRASES

Tanto-chokunyu
● 単刀直入

The originally meaning of the phrase was used for someone only armed with a single sword, who suprised the enemy with a single cut. Now it means that someone immediately grasps the important points of a situation.

7 Late-Muromachi Period
(15th to 16th C.)

By the late Muromachi period, fighting methods had changed from cavalry to mass infantry style warfare. The uchi-gatana became popular, worn with the cutting edge uppermost thrust through the sash. After the Onin, Bunmei disturbance, conflicts broke out in many places and kazu-uchi mono (mass-produced blades) began to appear. However, chumon-uchi (specially ordered blades of excellent quality) were also produced during this time. Bizen (p.65) and Mino (p.66) were the most prolific sites of production. The blades of this period are characterised by their strong saki-zori. During the Eisho and Tenbun eras, many rather short katate-uchi-gatana (for one-handed use) with a short nakago were produced. After these eras, sword production reverted back to swords for two-handed use. The blades also became wider with an extended chu-kissaki.

8 Azuchi-Momoyama Period
(late 16th C.)

Swords produced up to the Keicho era (1596-1614) are classified as Koto (old blades). Blades made during and after this era are classified as Shinto (new-swords). When Japan entered the Azuchi-Momoyama period, many smiths moved to Edo or Kyoto, or gathered in castle towns of various influential daimyo. Additionally, developments in transportation brought about experimentation with materials, and foreign-made steel (known as 'nanbantetsu') was utilized.

The blades shape from around this period mirrors that of shortened Nanbokucho blades (p.56). They are generally wide with little or no difference between the moto and saki-haba, have an extended chu-kissaki, or an o-kissaki. The difference from Nanbokucho blades is that the kasane is thicker on the Shinto blades.

In this era, men can be seen wearing flamboyant kimono with long swords thrust through their sash.

SHINTO PERIOD

9 Early-Edo Period (17th C.)

The swords of the early Edo-period are of a standard width. The saki-haba is relatively narrow when compared to the moto-haba, and the curvature becomes noticeably shallow. The point section also becomes small or a appears like a rather stunted chu-kissaki. Many are around 69.7 cm (2.3 shaku) in length.This shape is characteristic of workmanship around the Kanbun (1661-1673) and Enpo (1673-1681) eras. Therefore blades of this era are referred to as Kanbun-shinto.

Miyamoto Musashi was famous for his two-swords fighting style.

10 Mid-Edo Period
(17th to 18th C.)

The Jokyo (1684-1688) and Genroku (1688-1704) eras around the mid-Edo period reflects the peace that had spread across Japan as the numbers of smiths had decreased. The shape of swords also transitioned from the Kanbun-shinto shape to the shape of swords that mark the beginning of the Shin-shinto era of sword manufacture. As opposed to Kanbun-shinto blades, the kissaki become slightly extended and the curvature becomes quite deep.

MINI COLUMN

Kamon on Shinto Period Nakago

During this period, the eighth Tokugawa Shogun Yoshimune, encouraged the practice of martial arts. Satsuma swordsmiths Masakiyo and Yasuyo made swords in Edo and were permitted to carve a single Aoi (hollyhock) leaf mon onto their nakago. It can be said to have been an honor for the smiths. If we look further back, Echizen Yasutsugu was given the use of the character 'Yasu'(康) and permitted to use the triple hollyhock mon by the Shogun Tokugawa Ieyasu(家康). Furthermore, Inoue Shinkai of Osaka was given permission by the Imperial court to carve a 16-petal chrysanthemum crest into his tangs. The mon are carved into the nakago along with the smith's inscription

SHIN-SHINTO PERIOD

11 Bakumatsu Era
(The end of the Edo period, 19th C.)

Swords produced after the Meiwa era (1764-1772) are referred to as Shin-shinto (new, new-swords). During this period, many swords reflecting the tachi shapes of the Kamakura and Nanbokucho periods were produced. They have a thick kasane, but the hira-niku is not as full. The blades emulating the Kamakura period shape are of a similar width, or slightly more slender, with a chu-kissaki and a deep curvature. The blades recreated in a shortened Nanbokucho shape (p.56) are wide, with an extended chu-kissaki, or o-kissaki, and a shallow curvature.

SWORD RELATED
PHRASES

Denka no Hoto
● 伝家の宝刀

Swords are passed down as family treasures. They are usually not used, but can be brought out as a last resort.

12 Meiji Period Onwards

Blades made since the Haitorei edict (the banning of civilians from wearing swords) in 1876 until present day are referred to as gendaito (modern swords). Due to the Haitorei, the need for swords declined. However, in 1906 the craft gained imperial patronage. The swordsmiths Gassan Sadakazu and Miyamoto Kanenori were designated Tei-shitsu Gigei-in (craftsmen by Imperial appointment—equivalent to National Living Treasure). Since then, the swordsmith's craft has been preserved through the Meiji (1868-1912), Taisho (1912-1926), Showa (1926-1989) and Heisei (1989-) eras until today.

Today's swordsmiths try to recreate the workmanship of eminent smiths of every period, regardless of whether they worked in the Koto or Shinto eras of sword manufacture. In particular, Kamakura period tachi are a popular aim for many modern swordsmiths.

The *Gokaden*

● 五箇伝

*The Five Main Traditions
of Japanese Sword Making*

During the Koto period of sword making, there were prosperous centers of production with abundant resources of raw materials that were supported by the local manors, temples and the shogunate. The five provinces of Yamato (Nara prefecture), Yamashiro (Kyoto), Bizen (Okayama prefecture), Soshu (Kanagawa prefecture), and Mino (Gifu prefecture) all have very strong work characteristics. Each of these work styles has become a traditional style that has continued through the Shinto and Shin-shinto periods of sword manufacture until today. These five main styles are referred to as the Gokaden.

The Five Traditions of the Gokaden

During the Shinto and Shin-shinto eras, the location of sword manufacturing centers were affected by political and logistical factors causing Edo and Osaka to become centers of production. The makers would study by producing facsimile of works of all the Koto period traditional schools. This lead to a pursuit of their own independent styles of workmanship within those traditions. This way of manufacturing swords continues to this day.

64

Main Points
of the Gokaden

Yamato-den ● 大和伝

The Yamato tradition is thought to be the origin of all the traditions and therefore the oldest. However, the earliest extant verified signed work dates to the early-Kamakura period. There are five schools within the tradition: the Senjuin, Tegai, Taima, Shikkake and Hosho schools. The schools have strong ties to temples in Nara. The workmanship is rather austere.

◎ Characteristics
Blades have a high shinogi and masame can be seen in the hada.
The hamon are often nie-deki, suguha, and sunagashi, niju-ba kuichigai-ba activities are often seen.

Yamashiro-den ● 山城伝

The Yamashiro tradition reached its peak during the late-Heian period through to the late-Kamakura period. The main schools were the Sanjo, Gojo, Awataguchi and Rai schools. Many of their works display an elegance that reflects their proximity to the imperial court.

◎ Characteristics
The blades have a well-forged ko-itame hada with a gorgeous, lustrous jigane. The hamon is usually suguha based with ko-midare and ko-choji, with fine ko-nie in both the ji and the ha.

Bizen-den ● 備前伝

Swords in the Bizen tradition have been produced since the late-Heian period right through to present day. The most prolific tradition in terms of numbers of smith and swords, Bizen province is referred to as the mecca of swordmaking. Bizen province was rich in local materials, such as sand-iron and pine trees for charcoal. In the Koto period there were a number of schools centered around Osafune village competing with each other.

◎ Characteristics
The main characteristics of Bizen workmanship is a flamboyant, nioi-deki, overlapping choji (clove blossoms) hamon, and a prominent misty utsuri in the blade.

Soshu-den ● 相州伝

In the Kamakura period, the military government invited top smiths from around the country to Kamakura. Eventually, the master smith Masamune perfected the characteristic Soshu style of workmanship.

◎ Characteristics

The blades are ambitious in workmanship. They have an itame-hada with a notare-gunome hamon, exquisite nie, chikei, kinsuji in the ji and the ha. Soshu-den had a large effect on the other traditions.

Mino-den ● 美濃伝

Of the five traditions, Mino-den was the last to emerge and was mostly active between the Nanbokucho and late-Muromachi periods.

◎ Characteristics

The hada tends to be itame mixed with masame. The jigane has shirake (the steel has a whiteness). The hamon are gunome or prominent pointed togari-ba. Many Shinto works contain Mino characteristics. Seki city that was the center of Mino production during the Muromachi period still thrives today as a producer of swords, knives and edged tools.

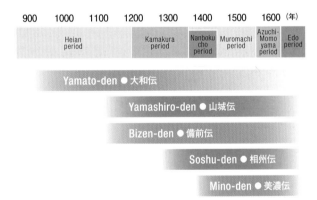

Progression chart of the Gokaden

Making
the Blade

As the name suggests, the Japanese sword is unique to Japan.
It is the pride of Japan,
known throughout the world as a fine steel work of art.
However, to meet its most basic function of a weapon
it must pass through various meticulous
production processes.

A Steel Production Method Unique to Japan:

Tatara

たたら

The raw materials for Japanese swords are produced by using the ancient Japanese method of steel production called Tatara. Due to this method, the quality of the steel is comparatively high. From the Meiji period onwards, Japan employed the western blast furnace technology of steel production. However, true Japanese swords cannot be made from western type steel.

Before the war, watetsu (traditional Japanese steel) was produced in small amounts in a place called Yasugi in Shimane prefecture. Nowadays, the Society for the Preservation of Japanese Art Swords manages the 'Nittoho Tatara' in Oku-Izumo village.

Charcoal and sand-iron are put into the clay furnace at thirty-minute intervals.

The Raw Materials of a Japanese Sword

A large block called a 'kera' is formed in the bottom of the Tatara (clay furnace). The block is broken up, the tamahagane is then selected by hand, and divided into three categories depending on the amount of carbon content. Among the groups classified as steel, the highest quality is tamahagane. This can be used in its original form to make swords. Zuku (pig-iron) is high in carbon content and requires decarburization to make swords.

Type	Carbon content	Characteristics
Iron ● 狭義の鉄	0.0 - 0.03%	Can be forged without heating
Steel ● 鋼	0.03 - 1.7%	Must be heated to be forged
Pig-iron ● 銑	1.7%	Difficult to forge even with heating

Tamahagane ● 玉鋼

Mizu-heshi and *Ko-wari*

THE JAPANESE SWORD MANUFACTURING PROCESS

MIZU-HESHI AND KO-WARI

TSUMI-WAKASHI

TANREN AND MAKING THE KAWAGANE

MAKING THE SHINGANE AND KUMI-AWASE

SUNOBE AND HI-ZUKURI

TSUCHI-OKI AND YAKI-IRE

FINISHING AND MEI-KIRI

● 水へし・小割り

The first process, mizu-heshi, begins by heating the tamahagane to a malleable temperature and then hammering it into a flat plate with a thickness of approximately 5 mm (fig. 1). The plate is then broken into 2-2.5 cm pieces (fig. 2). Next, the small wafers of tamahagane are separated into two groups (fig. 3): the kawagane (jacket-steel) and the shingane (core-steel).

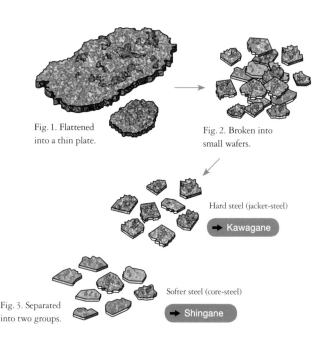

Fig. 1. Flattened into a thin plate.

Fig. 2. Broken into small wafers.

Hard steel (jacket-steel)
→ Kawagane

Softer steel (core-steel)
→ Shingane

Fig. 3. Separated into two groups.

70

Tsumi-wakashi

● 積沸し

An iron handle called a 'teko', is attached to a small plate of tamahagane (fig. 4), and the small wafers are stacked neatly onto the plate. The stack is then put into the swordsmith's hearth, heated and forged into a single block.

The wafers for the core-steel and the wafers for the jacket-steel are stacked onto seperate teko.

Fig. 4. Stacking the wafers onto the teko.

Tanren (forging) and Making the *Kawagane* (jacket-steel)

● 鍛錬・皮鉄造り

In order to remove any remaining impurities and evenly distribute the carbon content, the steel is repeatedly fold-forged. The billet is heated and hammered out into a rectangular shape. Then an incision is made and it is folded in half (fig. 5). This folding process is usually repeated about 15 times. However, the process is broken into two sections: shita-gitae (foundation forging) and age-gitae (finish forging).

This forging process produces the harder jacket-steel that wraps around the softer core-steel (fig. 6). Steel that has been folded 15 times has approximately 33,000 layers. This is one of the reasons that Japanese swords are so resilient.

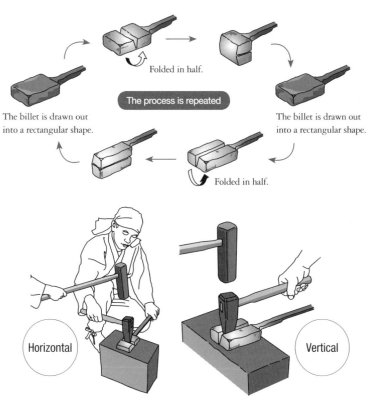

Folded in half.

The process is repeated

The billet is drawn out into a rectangular shape.

The billet is drawn out into a rectangular shape.

Folded in half.

Horizontal

Vertical

Fig. 5. An incision is made before it is folded in half.

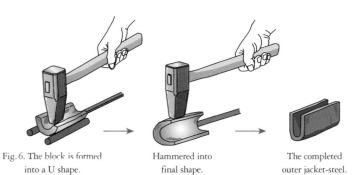

Fig. 6. The block is formed into a U shape.

Hammered into final shape.

The completed outer jacket-steel.

Making the *Shingane* (core-steel) and *Kumi-awase*
(inserting into the jacket-steel)

···

● 心鉄造り・組み合わせ

The core-steel can be made before or after the jacket steel (fig. 7). As Japanese swords must meet the three conditions of 'Not bending, not breaking, and cutting well', they must be resilient enough to hold a cutting edge, but not too brittle as they would break. To resolve this contradiction, the method of inserting a softer core-steel into a harder jacket steel was devised (fig. 8). This is the main characteristic of Japanese sword manufacture.

There are various methods of combining the softer and harder steels. Such as, makuri, kobuse, hon-sanmai, shiho-zume, etc. However, the methods vary according to period, schools, and individual swordsmiths.

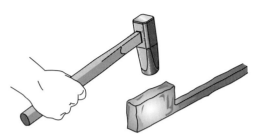

Fig. 7. The core-steel is hammered into shape.

The completed
core-steel.

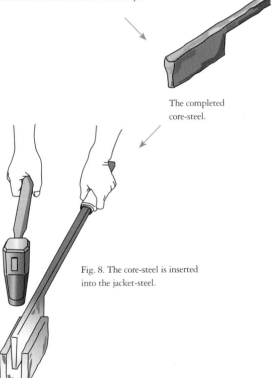

Fig. 8. The core-steel is inserted
into the jacket-steel.

Sunobe and *Hi-zukuri*

● 素延べ・火造り

Once the core-steel and jacket-steel have been successfully joined together, the billet is heated and hammered out into the shape of a long rectangular bar called a sunobe (fig. 9). When it has been hammered out to the required length for the sword, then the point section is formed.

Once the sunobe process is completed, the hi-zukuri process begins where the bar is then formed into the familiar shape of a Japanese sword using a small hammer (fig. 10), and the shape is refined using files to tailor the niku-oki (the geometry of the surface between the shinogi and the ha-saki).

Fig. 9. Hammering out into the shape of a long rectangular bar.

Forming the Kissaki (point section)

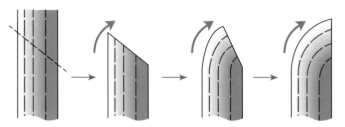

First, it is cut at an angle.　　　The point section is heated and formed using
a small hammer.

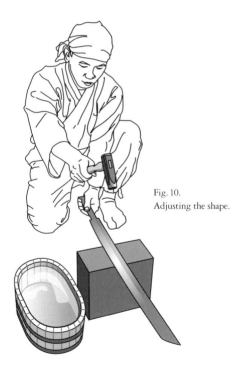

Fig. 10.
Adjusting the shape.

Tsuchi-oki and *Yaki-ire*
(clay application and quenching)

● 土置き・焼き入れ

The clay compound used as an insulator during the quenching process is mixed with fine charcoal powder and powdered polishing stone. It is applied to the blade to produce one of the types of hamon (fig. 11).

A thin layer of clay is applied along the cutting edge where it is to be hardened, and a thicker layer is applied to the back of the blade where it is to remain ductile. The swordsmith assesses the temperature of the blade by eye, heating it to about 800 degrees centigrade, and then quenching it into a bath of water (fig. 12).

Fig. 11. Applying the clay.

Fig. 12. Heating the blade.

Yaki-ire.
(quenching the blade)

Finishing and *Mei-kiri*
(signing the blade)

● 仕上げ・銘切り

Once the blade has been quenched, any warps or bends are adjusted, then using a rough whetstone, the smith refines the shape of the blade (fig. 13).

Lastly, after checking for any cracks or flaws in the blade, the nakago is finished, a hole is drilled for a retaining peg, and the maker adds his signature (fig. 14).

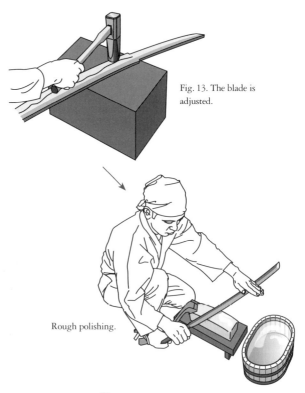

Fig. 13. The blade is adjusted.

Rough polishing.

80

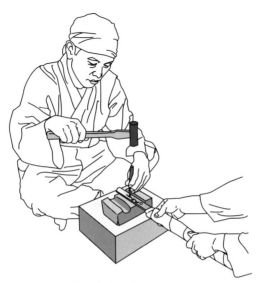

Fig. 14. The maker signs the blade.

Namakura

● 鈍ら

Means that a sword is blunt. The phrase is now used to mean that someone is a weakling, or someone who's skills have not yet fully developed.

The Craftsmen Involved with Making a Japanese Sword

The complicated processes involved in order to produce a single Japanese sword requires the skills of many craftsmen. Due to these sophisticated skills, the production of Japanese swords has been maintained since ancient times. For this reason, the Japanese sword is recognised as a culmination of all these crafts.

●**The main craftsmen**

Swordsmith .... Blade manufacture.
● 刀匠

Togi-shi .... Blade sharpening and polishing.
● 研師

Horimono-shi .... Decorative blade carvings.
● 刀身彫刻師

Shirogane-shi .... Mainly habaki production.
● 白銀師

Saya-shi .... Scabbard and mountings.
● 鞘師

Nu-shi .... Scabbard lacquering.
● 塗師

Tsukamaki-shi .... Applying ray-skin and wrapping the tsuka.
● 柄巻師

Kinko .... Fittings manufacture, tsuba, menuki, etc.
● 金工

The work may vary according to craftsman. These are just examples.

Polishing
the Blade

If the Japanese sword is not polished,
the secrets of its beauty will not be revealed.
Just like sword manufacture,
Japanese sword polishing has achieved
a high degree of progress.
It requires many meticulous processes to bring out
the blade's individual charm.

The Various Stages of Sword Polishing

The polishing of Japanese swords illuminates the grace and beauty of Japanese swords by revealing the characteristic lines of the blade, the forging patterns in the jigane (surface steel), and the exquisite hamon.

Togi-shi 研師

Shitaji-togi
(foundation polishing)

● 下地研ぎ

Polishing can be broken into two main stages: shitaji-togi and shiage-togi. Shitaji-togi mainly consists of refining the shape of the blade. Usually, six different types of polishing stones are used in the foundation polishing stage.

Various Grades of Polishing Stones

Stone	Place of origin		Grit factor*
Iyo-do ● 伊予砥	Matsuyama in Ehime prefecture	→	#400 grit
Binsui-do ● 備水砥	Amakusa in Kumamoto prefecture	→	#400 grit
Kaisei-do ● 改正砥	Yamagata prefecture	→	#600 grit
Nagura-do ● 名倉砥	Minami-Shitara, Aichi prefecture	→	#800-1200 grit
Koma-nagura-do ● 細名倉砥	Minami-Shitara, Aichi prefecture	→	#1500-2000 grit
Uchi-gumori-do ● 内曇砥	Kyoto	→	#4000-6000 grit

*The lower the number, the coarser the stone.

The uchigumori used to polish the hard section of the blade is called uchi-gumori ha-to, and the uchi-gumori used to polish the ji section of the blade is called uchi-gumori ji-to.

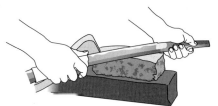

The polishing stones are matched to the condition and quality of the blade.

Shiage-togi
(finish polishing)

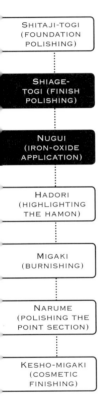

SHITAJI-TOGI
(FOUNDATION
POLISHING)

**SHIAGE-
TOGI (FINISH
POLISHING)**

**NUGUI
(IRON-OXIDE
APPLICATION)**

HADORI
(HIGHLIGHTING
THE HAMON)

MIGAKI
(BURNISHING)

NARUME
(POLISHING THE
POINT SECTION)

KESHO-MIGAKI
(COSMETIC
FINISHING)

● 仕上げ研ぎ

Once the foundation polishing stage is complete, the polisher moves on to the finish polishing stage. For this the hardened section of the blade (the cutting edge) is polished using hazuya, and the ji (body section of the blade) with jizuya. Hazuya is made from small pieces of wafer thin, good quality, uchi-gumori stone with yoshino-gami (paper) applied to the back using lacquer or glue.

Jizuya is made from very thin pieces of narutaki stone broken into even smaller pieces. Methods differ slightly according to polishing school, but generally this kind of polishing is performed using the thumb and a piece of jizuya crushed into 1 mm square pieces.

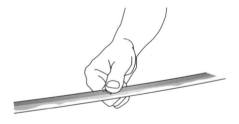

Refining the hada using jizuya.

Nugui
(iron-oxide application)

● 拭い

Once the finish polishing stage is complete, the next stage is to apply a compound called nugui. Nugui is used to give the blade luster. The method is often referred to as kanahada-nugui. Kanahada is an iron-oxide that accumulates around the anvil during forging. It is crushed into a fine powder and mixed with choji oil. Then, it is further refined by straining through yoshino-gami.

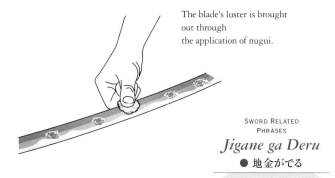

The blade's luster is brought out through
the application of nugui.

Hadori
(highlighting the hamon)

● 刃取り

Hadori is the process of whitening the hardened section of the blade to give it a beautiful appearance. This is performed using a wafer thin hazuya stone and a fine uchi-gumori slurry to highlight the shape of the hamon.

Hadori being performed using a thin hazuya stone.

SWORD RELATED
PHRASES
Kyuba-shinogi
● 急場凌ぎ

Kyuba was originally written with the characters for expedient and cutting edge. The meaning came from when a warrior's sword was damaged on the battlefield, he would use it regardless until the battle was done. Nowadays, it has come to mean to become resolute, and somehow struggle through a situation.

Migaki
(burnishing)

Once the hadori stage is complete, next the migaki stage begins. Migaki is the process when the blade is finished by burnishing the mune (spine), and shinogi-ji (the area between the spine and the ridgeline) with a metal burnishing rod, giving the areas a dark unique gloss.

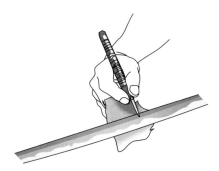

Migaki being performed with a burnishing rod.

Narume
(polishing the point section)

SHITAJI-TOGI
(FOUNDATION
POLISHING)

SHIAGE-
TOGI (FINISH
POLISHING)

NUGUI
(IRON-OXIDE
APPLICATION)

HADORI
(HIGHLIGHTING
THE HAMON)

MIGAKI
(BURNISHING)

NARUME
(POLISHING THE
POINT SECTION)

KESHO-MIGAKI
(COSMETIC
FINISHING)

● なるめ

Narume (polishing of the point section) is one of the final stages in sword polishing. Once the location of the yokote-suji is decided and applied, the final polishing of the point section begins. A piece of fine quality hazuya is set onto a special mount called a narume-dai. The point section is then polishing while taking special care to not damage the yokote-suji.

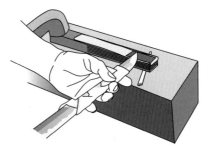

Finishing the point section using a narume-dai.

Kesho-migaki
(cosmetic finishing)

● 化粧磨き

After undergoing many stages in the polishing process, the very last stage is that of kesho-migaki. It is also sometimes referred to as the polishers signature. Kesho-migaki is a series of lines applied to the mune of the kissaki, and in the shinogi-ji at the habaki-moto by using a burnishing rod.

SWORD RELATED
PHRASES
Nuki Sashi Naranu
● 抜き差しならぬ

The case of when a blade becomes rusty and cannot be drawn from the saya. In other words, when a blade is drawn great care should be taken before it is put away. Nowadays, the phrase means to be in a tough or 'sticky' situation.

Japanese Sword Care and Maintenance

In general, to preserve the blade and stop it from rusting it should be kept lightly oiled in a shirasaya (p.98). The blade should be cleaned and re-oiled every few months. The old oil should be removed as much as possible, and a thin layer of new oil applied over the whole blade.

These are the basic tools required for sword maintenance.

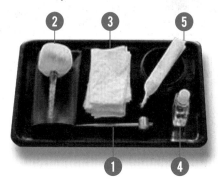

❶ *Mekugi-nuki* ● 目釘抜

A tool used to remove the bamboo retaining peg from the handle of the sword. Mekugi-nuki are usually made of either brass or bamboo.

❷ *Uchiko* ● 打粉

Uchiko is very finely ground particles of polishing stone wrapped in a yoshino-gami cotton and silk ball. When the ball is tapped lightly on the blade very finely filtered stone powder is applied onto the blade.

❸ *Nugui-gami* ● 拭い紙

A high quality, soft, traditional Japanese paper used to wipe dirt and particles from the blade. It is important that one sheet is used for old oil removal, and a separate sheet is used to remove the applied uchiko powder. In the case that soft brushed cotton cloth is to be used in place of nugui-gami, make sure that it has been washed thoroughly, and is completely dry before using.

❹ Oil ● 油

A light oil called choji oil is applied to the blade to protect it from rusting.

❺ Oil applicator ● 油塗紙

An appropriate sized piece of soft brushed cotton cloth or nugui-gami used to apply the oil to the blade.

Sword Fittings and Mountings

The mountings and fittings that are constructed
to mount the blade must be easy to use.
They are generally referred to as koshirae (mountings) and
tosogu (sword fittings). Koshirae are the external arts
of the Japanese sword. As well as being practical,
there many designs involving much technology.
The various parts of the koshirae
are all made by different specialist craftsmen.
A completed koshirae is the culmination of the work
of these very skilled craftsmen.

Sword Fittings and Mountings

A complete mounting furnished with fittings is referred to as a koshirae. In this section we will look at tachi and uchi-gatana koshirae, and the various types of fittings.

Koshirae

● 拵

There are different types of koshirae, such as tachi koshirae or uchi-gatana koshirae. However, the blades that are housed inside come in all different shapes. The placing of the fittings may be the same, but according to period and types, the names of the parts can change.

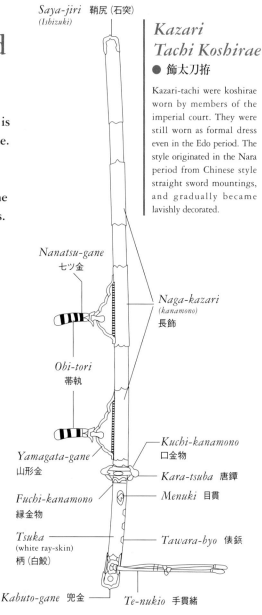

Saya-jiri 鞘尻 〔石突〕
(Ishizuki)

Nanatsu-gane
七ツ金

Obi-tori
帯執

Yamagata-gane
山形金

Fuchi-kanamono
縁金物

Tsuka
(white ray-skin)
柄 (白鮫)

Kabuto-gane 兜金

Naga-kazari
(kanamono)
長飾

Kuchi-kanamono
口金物

Kara-tsuba 唐鐔

Menuki 目貫

Tawara-byo 俵鋲

Te-nukio 手貫緒

Kazari Tachi Koshirae

● 飾太刀拵

Kazari-tachi were koshirae worn by members of the imperial court. They were still worn as formal dress even in the Edo period. The style originated in the Nara period from Chinese style straight sword mountings, and gradually became lavishly decorated.

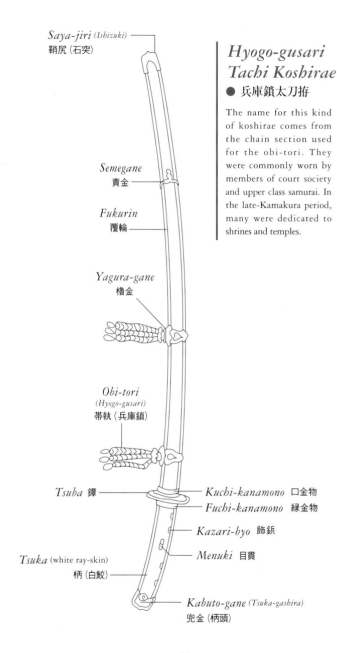

Saya-jiri (Ishizuki)
鞘尻（石突）

Hyogo-gusari
Tachi Koshirae
● 兵庫鎖太刀拵

The name for this kind
of koshirae comes from
the chain section used
for the obi-tori. They
were commonly worn by
members of court society
and upper class samurai. In
the late-Kamakura period,
many were dedicated to
shrines and temples.

Semegane
責金

Fukurin
覆輪

Yagura-gane
櫓金

Obi-tori
(Hyogo-gusari)
帯執（兵庫鎖）

Tsuba 鐔

Kuchi-kanamono 口金物
Fuchi-kanamono 縁金物

Kazari-byo 飾鋲

Menuki 目貫

Tsuka (white ray-skin)
柄（白鮫）

Kabuto-gane (Tsuka-gashira)
兜金（柄頭）

Ito-maki Tachi Koshirae

● 糸巻太刀拵

The handle and the upper part of the saya are covered in gold brocade, and wrapped with cord. The saya are often decorated with lacquer designs. Samurai family crests (kamon) were often applied for ceremonial and battle identification purposes in the 16th to 18th centuries.

Upper class samurai were obligated to offer ito-maki tachi to shrines and temples as gifts or offerings.

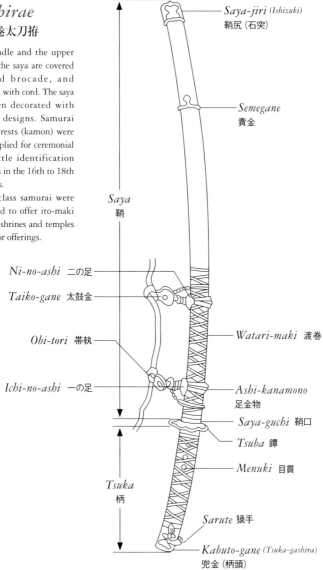

Saya-jiri (Ishizuki)
鞘尻 (石突)

Semegane
責金

Saya
鞘

Ni-no-ashi 二の足

Taiko-gane 太鼓金

Obi-tori 帯執

Ichi-no-ashi 一の足

Watari-maki 渡巻

Ashi-kanamono
足金物

Saya-guchi 鞘口

Tsuba 鐔

Menuki 目貫

Tsuka
柄

Sarute 猿手

Kabuto-gane (Tsuka-gashira)
兜金 (柄頭)

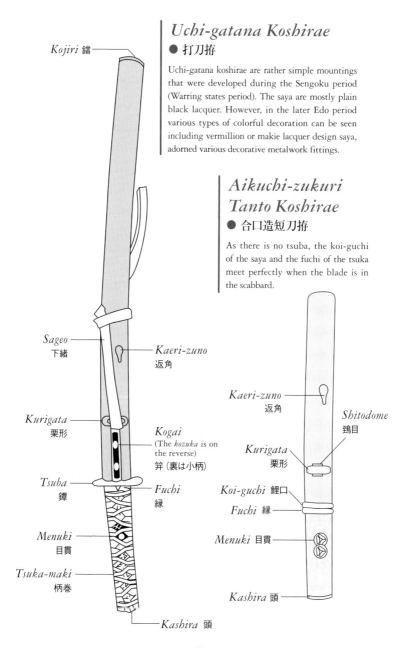

Kojiri 鐺

Uchi-gatana Koshirae
● 打刀拵

Uchi-gatana koshirae are rather simple mountings that were developed during the Sengoku period (Warring states period). The saya are mostly plain black lacquer. However, in the later Edo period various types of colorful decoration can be seen including vermillion or makie lacquer design saya, adorned various decorative metalwork fittings.

Aikuchi-zukuri Tanto Koshirae
● 合口造短刀拵

As there is no tsuba, the koi-guchi of the saya and the fuchi of the tsuka meet perfectly when the blade is in the scabbard.

Sageo
下緒

Kaeri-zuno
返角

Kaeri-zuno
返角

Shitodome
鵐目

Kurigata
栗形

Kogai
(The *kozuka* is on the reverse)
笄（裏は小柄）

Kurigata
栗形

Tsuba
鐔

Fuchi
縁

Koi-guchi 鯉口

Fuchi 縁

Menuki
目貫

Menuki 目貫

Tsuka-maki
柄巻

Kashira 頭

Kashira 頭

Saya (scabbard) ● 鞘

When a blade is worn or transported, it is stored in a saya. Very old saya were made from cow-skin or bamboo, but soon after many began to be constructed from honoki (magnolia wood). Initially, these saya were thin in construction and were called hirazaya.

Later, thicker, leather wrapped, and lacquered saya became widely used. In the medieval period, expensive tachi-koshirae with gilt bronze or silver fittings came into use. Additionally, there were nishiki-tsutsumi saya (brocade), hiru-maki saya (saya wrapped in strips of metal), and tomaki-saya (rattan). Tachi-koshirae of the Edo period commonly have saya with a nashiji or ikakeji lacquer, with raden or maki-e designs.

Early modern uchi-gatana, wakizashi and tanto koshirae are generally lacquered. A samurai's formal daisho would have plain black lacquered saya (p.15). From the mid-Edo period onwards, there was a demand for variation in saya lacquering, and many new lacquering methods were developed (p.108).

As the lacquering techniques were made full use of, the skills were taken to a very high level. In order to preserve the blades and the koshirae, the blade is removed and put into a plain wooden sleeping scabbard called a shirasaya. Shirasaya are made from honoki. Compared to other woods, honoki is an easy to work, soft wood that is low in oils.

Sori ga Awanai
● 反りが合わない

Every single sword's
curvature is slightly different
to each other. As the saya
are custom made to fit each
sword, the sword will not fit
into another sword's saya.
When things or people are
incompatible, the phrase
"Sori ga awanai!" is used.

Moto no Saya ni Osamaru
● 元の鞘に納まる

*"Moto no saya ni
osameru"* means to
returning a sword to
its original saya. This
phrase is used when
two people reconcile
after a disagreement.

Tsuka ● 柄

The tsuka is the handle of the sword. From the early modern period onwards honoki (magnolia wood) is used for the handle's core, and wrapped in ray-skin. It is then wrapped tightly with ito (cord) in hishi-ito-maki (a diamond shaped pattern). In the past, citrus and hardwoods were used. In ancient times, rhinoceros horn, rosewood, agarwood, dark persimmon, zelkova, and redwood were wrapped and used.

The swords of the Imperial court nobles and guards were not wrapped with cord. However, the warrior class had utilitarian leather and cord wrapped handles. Around the time of the Warring States period, ray-skin wrapped handles bound with cord became standard. Ray-skin was also lacquered black to withstand inclement weather. Tsuka were also wrapped in leather, baleen, hemp, and various types of braid.

The handle is wrapped using a flat braided cord. Among the common methods used to wrap the handle are: tsumami-maki (the cord is pinched at the point where it crosses over), hineri-maki (the cord is twisted at the point where it crosses over to create tension), and hira-maki (the cord remains flat at the point where it crosses over). There are also many other different wrapping methods.

Examples of Types of Tsuka-maki (handle wraps)

Tsuka-maki begins at the fuchi and ends with a knot just below the kashira.
Tachi koshirae are wrapped in hira-maki, whereas uchi-gatana koshirae are
often wrapped in hineri or tsumami-maki.

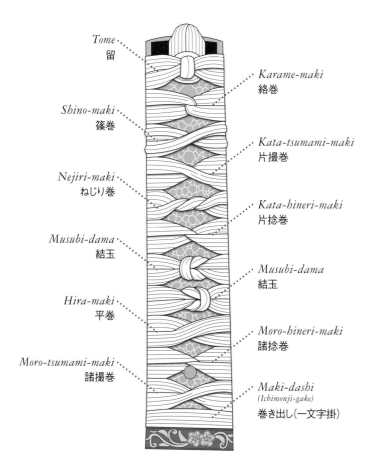

Tome
留

Karame-maki
絡巻

Shino-maki
篠巻

Kata-tsumami-maki
片撮巻

Nejiri-maki
ねじり巻

Kata-hineri-maki
片捻巻

Musubi-dama
結玉

Musubi-dama
結玉

Hira-maki
平巻

Moro-hineri-maki
諸捻巻

Moro-tsumami-maki
諸撮巻

Maki-dashi
(Ichimonji-gake)
巻き出し(一文字掛)

Habaki ● 鎺

The habaki is positioned at the base of the blade between the nakago and the blade proper. The habaki fits into the koi-guchi in such a way, that the blade makes very little contact with the inside of the scabbard.

There are different styles of habaki for tachi and katana. Very old tachi habaki would be affixed by sliding on from the tip of the blade and then fixed at the habaki-moto. Later, all habaki were made so as to be mounted onto the blade from the nakago end.

Originally, habaki were made from iron by the swordsmith himself. These iron habaki are referred to as tomo-habaki and are highly prized.

Many tachi habaki do not have a slot at the mune, whereas katana habaki do have a slot. Habaki come in one (hitoe) or two pieces (futae, or niju-habaki). Many Koto blades have two piece habaki, and many Shinto blades are seen with single (one piece) habaki. In the Edo period it was commonplace to have a plain copper habaki. However, Daimyo family swords and masterpieces would have silver or gold habaki.

Since the modern era, ornate gold habaki have become popular. As they are now made from metals other than iron, they are mainly made by a shirogane-shi (silversmith).

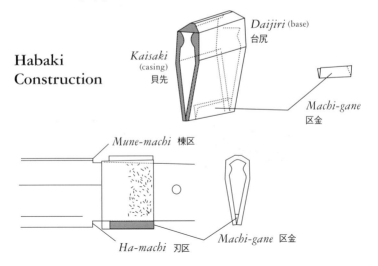

Habaki Construction

Kaisaki (casing) 貝先

Daijiri (base) 台尻

Machi-gane 区金

Mune-machi 棟区

Ha-machi 刃区

Machi-gane 区金

Types of Habaki

Tachi Habaki
● 太刀鎺

There is no slot in the top, and they are commonly made with vertical filemarks.

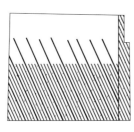

Hitoe-habaki
● 一重鎺

A one piece habaki. These are made with various types of colored metals and filemarks.

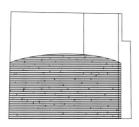

Futae-habaki
● 二重鎺

A habaki made from two pieces. An upper piece is encased by the lower piece.

Tsuba ● 鐔

There are different tsuba for tachi and katana. The nakago-hitsu-ana has the cutting edge side uppermost with tachi tsuba, and facing downwards with katana tsuba.

Tachi tsuba are often used on tachi koshirae from since before the Muromachi period. They were originally made of thick layers of hardened leather secured together with a fukurin. Tsuba come in various other materials, gilt bronze, or large, thin iron-plate with a thick fukurin, or with o-seppa (large seppa).

From the Momoyama period onwards (late 16th C.), mostly katana tsuba were used. Tachi tsuba were used for ito-maki tachi koshirae, for ceremonial and official events. There is a variety of katana tsuba that are all named after their locations of manufacture, the school of the maker, base materials, or makers names. From the Edo period onwards the use of various colored metals, and specialist carving techniques were greatly employed. Many master craftsmen came to the fore, producing more carved tsuba than any other fitting.

Types of Tsuba and their Terminology

Tachi Tsuba
● 太刀鐔

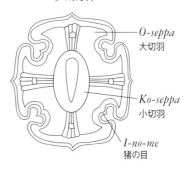

O-seppa 大切羽

Ko-seppa 小切羽

I-no-me 猪の目

Katana Tsuba
● 刀鐔

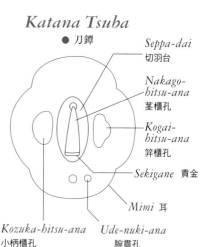

Seppa-dai 切羽台

Nakago-hitsu-ana 茎櫃孔

Kogai-hitsu-ana 笄櫃孔

Sekigane 責金

Mimi 耳

Kozuka-hitsu-ana 小柄櫃孔

Ude-nuki-ana 腕貫孔

Various Tsuba Shapes

Maru-gata
(rounded)
● 丸形

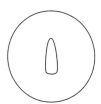

Kikka-gata
(chrysanthemum)
● 菊花形

Nadekaku-gata
(square with rounded corners)
● 撫角形

Mokko-gata
(four lobed)
● 木瓜形

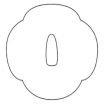

Aori-gata
(egg-shaped)
● 障泥形

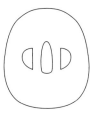

SWORD RELATED
PHRASES

Seppa Tsumaru
● 切羽詰まる

Seppa are a kind of washer that fit between the fuchi and the tsuba, and between the tsuba and the habaki to stop the tsuba from moving and rattling. When used in conversation, it means that someone is trapped in a certain situation.

Kozuka, Kogai and *Menuki*

● 小柄・笄・目貫

Among the fittings, the kozuka, kogai and menuki are collectively referred to as mi-tokoro-mono. It is common for these three items to be made as a set.

Nowadays, the kozuka are referred to as paper-knife. However, in the Edo period they were called 'kogatana-tsuka'. A kogai is said to be a tool for fixing a samurai's hair, and the small scoop on the end is used for cleaning the ears. Menuki developed from retaining pegs to decorative fittings used to stop the handle from sliding through the hands. Mi-tokoro-mono were always attached to samurai's formal daisho mountings and presentation mountings. The founder of the Goto school of fittings makers, Goto Yujo, served the eighth Ashikaga shogun Yoshimasa. Subsequent generations were in the employ of the Toyotomi family and Tokugawa shogunal family. As a result, the Goto family works are referred to as Ie-bori, and fittings made by craftsmen for the general public are referred to as Machi-bori carvers.

SWORD RELATED
PHRASES

Menuki-dori

● 目抜き(目貫)通り

Located on the tsuka, menuki are the most eye catching feature. This phrase later came to mean the main street in a town.

Parts of a Kozuka

Parts of a Kogai

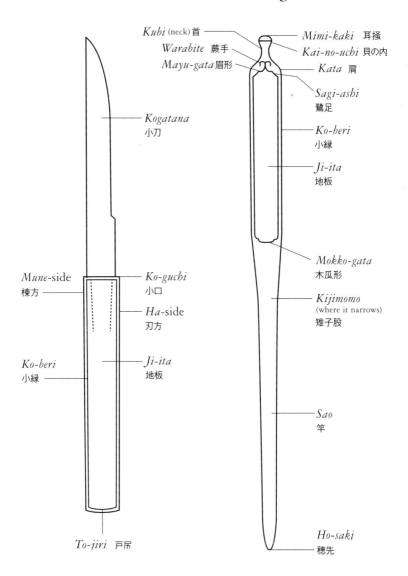

Kubi (neck) 首

Warabite 蕨手

Mayu-gata 眉形

Kogatana 小刀

Mune-side 棟方

Ko-guchi 小口

Ha-side 刃方

Ko-beri 小縁

Ji-ita 地板

To-jiri 戸尻

Mimi-kaki 耳掻

Kai-no-uchi 貝の内

Kata 肩

Sagi-ashi 鷺足

Ko-beri 小縁

Ji-ita 地板

Mokko-gata 木瓜形

Kijimomo (where it narrows) 雉子股

Sao 竿

Ho-saki 穂先

Saya Lacquering

The lacquering of saya is one aspect of sword mountings. It has been performed since the Nara period (710-794), and is still done today. Layers of Japanese urushi are applied to both decorate and protect the saya. Samurai of the Edo period were required to wear matching sets of long and short swords with plain black lacquered scabbards on formal occasions. However, at the same time, there were also many different, stylish types of saya using various lacquering techniques.

● *Shibo-urushi*

Urushi (Japanese lacquer) is mixed with small amounts of tofu (soya bean curd), mana-fu (wheat gluten) and egg-white to increase drying and adhesion. Lacquering styles include Isokusa-nuri and Shigure-nuri.

● Foundation Lacquering

To prepare for a distinctive foundation, lacquer is mixed with powered stone. This makes it possible to make large raised designs. Lacquering styles include Matsukawa-nuri, Sakuragawa-nuri and Take-nuri (bamboo) .

● Seeds and Leaves

After a layer of lacquer has been applied to the saya, seed or leaves such as, rapeseed, rice husks, palm fiber, and shredded tobacco are adhered, before the final lacquering process is completed. Lacquering styles include Nanako-nuri and Shuroge-nuri.

● *Togidashi*

The base color lacquer is covered by a different top coat color. The top coat is then polished away, exposing patches of the base coat. Lacquering styles include Shu-mijin nuri, Shitan-nuri and Danmon-nuri.

● *Suiage*

Before the lacquer is fully hardened designs are drawn into the surface, creating elevations in the lacquer. Lacquering styles include Yozakura-nuri and Nunome-nuri.

● *Fun-maki*

The surface of the saya is lacquered. The dried layer is then sprinkled with powered lacquer or charcoal before the final layer is applied. Lacquering styles include Ishime-nuri and Tetsu-sabi-nuri.

● Egg-shell and *Aogai* (limpet shell)

Powered egg-shell or aogai is sprinkled onto the surface. A final coat is applied to bring out the design. Lacquering styles include Rankaku-nuri and Aogai mijin-nuri.

Japanese Sword Appraisal

Sword Appraisal History

It is thought that the appreciation and discernment of Japanese swords began at the same time as the birth of Japanese swords themselves. According to old documents, 'sword appraisal' was popularised during the Muromachi period by the appraiser Amishu(阿弥衆)*. Hon'ami Kotoku, who served Toyotomi Hideyoshi, was able to appraise unsigned swords and verify the makers. He also began the practice of inlaying gold inscriptions into unsigned swords attributing the work to a particular maker. The Hon'ami family served successive Shoguns, and Daimyo class families. In the Edo period, they were permitted by the Edo goverment to issue sword appraisal papers referred to as 'origami'. In the world of sword fittings, the Ie-bori Goto family (p.106) issued appraisal certificates authenticating the works of previous generations of the family. From these certificates comes the saying that a work 'has papers', meaning that a sword or fittings have been verified as a particular person, or school's workmanship.

From the Meiji period onwards, the practice of origami was popularised by appraisers and enthusiasts, and transitioned into kantei-sho (certificates of authenticity) and sayagaki (attributions written directly onto a shirasaya). The practice still continues to this day.

*The appellation 'ami' was used from the Muromachi period onwards for various entertainment people close to the Shogun. In recent history, the Hon'ami were the main issuers of sword appraisal certificates, however, there are also extant sword documents by the Ki'ami, and No'ami families.

How Appraisal is Performed

The first step in actually appraising a sword is to check whether the signature (if it has one) is genuine. Next, check to make sure that the period and province of manufacture, match the workmanship of the smith.

In the case of unsigned swords, the shape is checked against its current condition. If it has been shortened, try to assume its original shape. Then decide if it is Koto or Shinto, and try to assess its period of manufacture. Next, by looking at the hamon and the jigane, try to narrow the workmanship down to a province, school, or maker. If much evidence presents itself, an attribution to a school or maker is made.

The appraisal of sword fittings and mountings is fundamentally the same. The shape and the condition is compared to the era and the workmanship. In the case of signed fittings, the signature is examined and compared against known examples. In the case of unsigned works, they are thoroughly researched.

An origami for a Koto blade by Norishige of Etchu province (Toyama prefecture).

An origami for a Kozuka by the 2nd Generation head of the Goto family, Sojo.

The *Goki-Shichido* ● 五畿七道

The Goki-shichido are ancient administrative divisions of the five prefectures surrounding the Kyoto imperial court, and the seven main roads of Japan. Technology and culture would travel along these roads. Even with the changes in history, movement of the swordsmiths, schools, and workmanship styles can be seen to travel along these routes.

Settsu 摂津
Yamashiro 山城
Kawachi 河内
Izumi 和泉
Yamato 大和

Goki ● 五畿

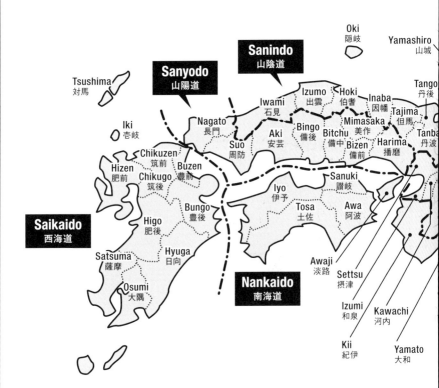

Oki 隠岐
Yamashiro 山城

Sanindo 山陰道

Sanyodo 山陽道

Tsushima 対馬

Tango 丹後

Izumo 出雲
Hoki 伯耆
Inaba 因幡
Tajima 但馬
Iwami 石見

Iki 壱岐

Nagato 長門

Aki 安芸
Bingo 備後
Mimasaka 美作
Tanba 丹波
Bitchu 備中
Bizen 備前
Harima 播磨

Chikuzen 筑前
Suo 周防

Hizen 肥前
Buzen 豊前
Chikugo 筑後

Iyo 伊予
Sanuki 讃岐

Saikaido 西海道

Bungo 豊後

Higo 肥後
Tosa 土佐
Awa 阿波

Satsuma 薩摩
Hyuga 日向

Awaji 淡路

Nankaido 南海道

Osumi 大隅

Settsu 摂津

Izumi 和泉
Kawachi 河内

Kii 紀伊
Yamato 大和

112

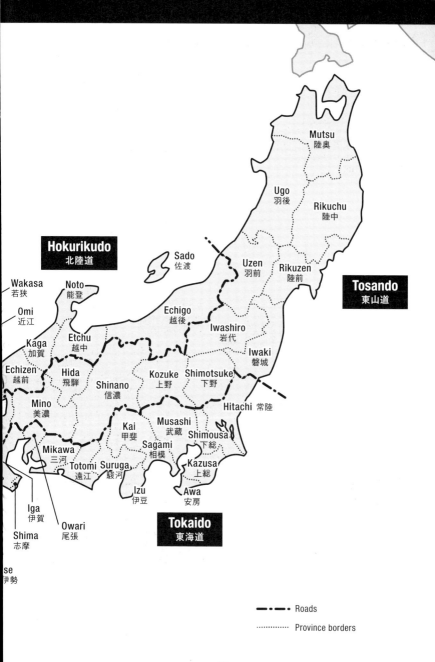

Mutsu
陸奥

Ugo
羽後

Rikuchu
陸中

Hokurikudo
北陸道

Sado
佐渡

Uzen
羽前

Rikuzen
陸前

Tosando
東山道

Wakasa
若狭

Noto
能登

Omi
近江

Echigo
越後

Iwashiro
岩代

Kaga
加賀

Etchu
越中

Echizen
越前

Hida
飛騨

Iwaki
磐城

Mino
美濃

Shinano
信濃

Kozuke
上野

Shimotsuke
下野

Hitachi 常陸

Kai
甲斐

Musashi
武蔵

Shimousa
下総

Mikawa
三河

Sagami
相模

Kazusa
上総

Totomi Suruga
遠江 駿河

Iga
伊賀

Izu
伊豆

Awa
安房

Owari
尾張

Tokaido
東海道

Shima
志摩

se
伊勢

—·—·—· Roads

············· Province borders

113

Mainline Schools and Smiths

KOTO PERIOD ●古刀

Kinai ●畿内	**Yama shiro** ●山城	Sanjo Munechika 三条宗近 Sanjo Yoshiie 三条吉家 Gojo Kanenaga 五条兼永 　Gojo Kuninaga 五条国永 Ayanokoji Sadatoshi 綾小路定利 Awataguchi school 粟田口系 ● Kunitomo 国友 Kunitsuna 国綱 Norikuni 則国 　Kuniyoshi 国吉 Yoshimitsu 吉光 Rai school 来系 ● Rai Kuniyuki 来国行 Niji Kunitoshi 国俊 Rai Kunitoshi 来国俊 　Rai Kunimitsu 来国光 Rai Kunitsugu 来国次 Rai Mitsukane 来光包 Hasebe school 長谷部系 ● Kunishige 国重 Kuninobu 国信 Kunihira 国平 Ryokai 了戒 Ryo Hisanobu 了久信 Nobukuni 信国 Heianjo Nagayoshi 平安城長吉 Sanjo Yoshinori 三条吉則
	Yamato ●大和	Senjuin school 千手院系 Taima school 当麻系 (Kuniyuki 国行) Shikkake school 尻懸系 (Norinaga 則長) Ryumon school 龍門系 (Nobuyoshi 延吉) Tegai school 手掻系 ● Kanenaga 包永 Kanekiyo 包清 Kaneuji 包氏 Hosho school 保昌系 ● Sadamune 貞宗 Sadayoshi 貞吉 Sadaoki 貞興 Kanabo 金房
Tokaido ●東海道	**Musashi** ●武蔵	Shitahara school 下原系 ● Yasushige 康重 Chikashige 周重 Terushige 照重
	Sagami ●相模	Shintogo Kunimitsu 新藤五国光 Yukimitsu 行光 Masamune 正宗 Sadamune 貞宗 Hiromitsu 広光 Akihiro 秋広 Masahiro 正広 Hiromasa 広正 Hirotsugu 広次 Fusamune 総宗 Tsunahiro 綱広 Yasuharu 康春
	Suruga ●駿河	Shimada school 島田系 ● Gisuke 義助 Sukemune 助宗 Hirosuke 広助
	Ise ●伊勢	Muramasa 村正 Masashige 正重
Tosando ●東山道	**Mutsu** ●陸奥	Gassan 月山 Hoju 宝寿
	Mino ●美濃	Shizu Kaneuji 志津兼氏 Naoe Shizu school 直江志津系 ● Kanetsugu 兼次 　Kanetomo 兼友 Kanenobu 兼信 Kanemoto 兼元 Kanesada 兼定 Kanetsune 兼常 Kaneyoshi 兼吉 Kanekuni 兼国 (Sue-Seki) Kinju 金重 Kingyo 金行 Daido 大道 Ujifusa 氏房 Ujisada 氏貞

	Omi ●近江	Takagi Sadamune 高木貞宗 Kanro Toshinaga 甘呂俊長
Hokurikudo ●北陸道	**Echigo** ●越後	Momokawa Nagayoshi 桃川長吉 Yamamura Masanobu 山村正信
	Etchu ●越中	Yoshihiro 義弘 Norishige 則重 Tametsugu 為継 Uda school 宇多系 ● Kunifusa 国房 Kunimitsu 国光 Kunimune 国宗
	Kaga ●加賀	Sanekage 真景 Fujishima Tomoshige 藤島友重 Katsuie 勝家 Ietsugu 家次 Kagemitsu 景光 Kiyomitsu 清光
	Echizen ●越前	Chiyozuru school 千代鶴系 ● Kuniyasu 国安 Morihiro 守弘
	Wakasa ●若狭	Fuyuhiro 冬広
Sanindo ●山陰道	**Tajima** ●但馬	Kunimitsu 国光
	Inaba ●因幡	Kagenaga 景長 Yukikage 行景
	Hoki ●伯耆	Yasutsuna 安綱 Ohara Sanemori 大原真守 Hiroyoshi 広賀
	Izumo ●出雲	Tadasada 忠貞
	Iwami ●石見	Naotsuna 直綱 Sadatsuna 貞綱 Sadayuki 貞行 Sadasue 貞末 Yoshisue 祥末
Sanyodo ●山陽道	**Bizen** ●備前	Ko-Bizen school 古備前系 ● Tomonari 友成 Masatsune 正恒 Ko-Ichimonji school 古一文字系 ● Norimune 則宗 Sukemune 助宗 Narimune 成宗 Ichimonji school 一文字系 ● 　Fukuoka 福岡 Yoshioka 吉岡 Katayama 片山 Shochu 正中 schools 　Yoshifusa 吉房 Sukezane 助真 Norifusa 則房 Yoshihira 吉平 　Sukeyoshi 助吉 Sukemitsu 助光 Osafune Mainline school 長船嫡系 ● 　Mitsutada 光忠 Nagamitsu 長光 Kagemitsu 景光 Other Osafune smiths 長船傍系 ● Sanenaga 真長 Chikakage 近景 Motoshige 元重 Hatakeda school 畠田系 ● Moriie 守家 Sanemori 真守 Unrui school 雲類系 ● Unsho 雲生 Unji 雲次 Unju 雲重 Chogi (Nagayoshi) school 長義系 ● 　Nagayoshi 長義 Kanenaga 兼長 Nagashige 長重 Nagamori 長守 Yoshii school 吉井系 ● Kagenori 景則 Kiyonori 清則 Yoshinori 吉則 Omiya school 大宮系 ● Morikage 盛景 Kozori school 小反物 ● Hidemitsu 秀光 Naruie 成家

● Sanyodo **● 山陽道**	**Bizen** **●備前**	Oei Bizen 応永備前 ● Morimitsu 盛光 Yasumitsu 康光 Eikyo Bizen 永享備前 ● Norimitsu 則光 Sukemitsu 祐光 Sue Bizen 末備前 ● Munemitsu 宗光 Katsumitsu 勝光 Sukesada 祐定
	Bitchu **●備中**	Masatsune 正恒 Sadatsugu 貞次 Yasutsugu 康次 Moritsugu 守次 Yoshitsugu 吉次 Naotsugu 直次 Tsugunao 次直 Tsuguyoshi 次吉
	Bingo **●備後**	Ko-Mihara school 古三原系 ● Masaie 正家 Masahiro 正広 Sue-Mihara 末三原 Kai-Mihara 貝三原 Hokke Ichijo 法華一乗
	Suo **●周防**	Nio Kiyotsuna 二王清綱 Kiyohisa 清久
	Nagato **●長門**	Yasuyoshi 安吉 (Choshu-Sa 長州左) Akikuni 顕国
● Nankaido **● 南海道**	**Kii** **●紀伊**	Iruga 入鹿 Sudo Kunitsugu 簑戸国次
	Awa **●阿波**	Kaifu school 海部系 ● Ujiyasu 氏泰 Ujiyoshi 氏吉
	Tosa **●土佐**	Yoshimitsu 吉光
● Saikaido **● 西海道**	**Chikuzen** **●筑前**	Ryosai 良西 Jitsua 実阿 Sairen 西蓮 Sa school 左系 ● Yasuyoshi 安吉 Yukihiro 行弘 Hiroyasu 弘安 Yoshisada 吉貞 Kongohyoe Moritaka 金剛兵衛盛高
	Chikugo **●筑後**	Miike Tenta Mitsuyo 三池典太光世 Oishi-Sa Ienaga 大石左 家永 Sukenaga 資永
	Buzen **●豊前**	Choen 長円 Chikushi Nobukuni 筑紫信国
	Bungo **●豊後**	Sadahide 定秀 Yukihira 行平 Takada Tomoyuki 高田友行 Tokiyuki 時行 Chikushi Ryokai 筑紫了戒 Yoshisada 能定
	Hizen **●肥前**	Hirado-Sa 平戸左
	Higo **●肥後**	Enju school 延寿系 ● Kunimura 国村 Kunisuke 国資 Kunitoki 国時 Kuniyoshi 国吉 Dotanuki Masakuni 同田貫正国 Kozuke-no-suke 上野介
	Satsuma **●薩摩**	Naminohira Yukiyasu 波平行安 Yasuie 安家

Kinai ●畿内	**Kyoto** ●京都	Umetada Myoju 埋忠明寿 Higashiyama Yoshihira 東山美平 Horikawa school 堀川系 ● Kunihiro 国広 Kuniyasu 国安 Kunitomo 国儔 Masahiro 正弘 Kunimichi 国路 Mishina school 三品系 ● Iga no Kami Kinmichi 伊賀守金道 Tanba no Kami Yoshimichi 丹波守吉道 Etchu no Kami Masatoshi 越中守正俊 Omi no Kami Hisamichi 近江守久道 Tango no Kami Kanemichi 丹後守兼道 Nankai Taro Tomotaka 南海太郎朝尊 Chigusa Arikoto 千種有功 Komai Keinin 駒井慶任
	Osaka ●大坂	Kunisada school 国貞系 ● Izumi no Kami Kunisada 和泉守国貞 Inoue Shinkai 井上真改 The Sukehiro school 助広系 ● Echizen no Kami Sukehiro 越前守助広 Omi no Kami Sukenao 近江守助直 The Kanesada school 包貞系 ● Echizen no Kami Kanesada 越前守包貞 Sakakura Terukane 坂倉照包 (2nd Gen.Kanesada 包貞) Kunisuke school 国助系 ● Kawachi no Kami Kunisuke 河内守国助 Ise no Kami Kuniteru 伊勢守国輝 Higo no Kami Kuniyasu 肥後守国康 Tadatsuna school 忠綱系 ● Omi no Kami Tadatsuna 近江守忠綱 Ikkanshi Tadatsuna 一竿子忠綱 Ishido school 石堂系 ● Tatara Choko (Nagayuki) 多々良長幸 Gassan school 月山系 ● Gassan Sadayoshi 月山貞吉 Sadakazu 貞一 Ozaki Suketaka 尾崎助隆 Masataka 正隆
	Yamato ●大和	Tsutsui Kiju 筒井紀充
Tokaido ●東海道	**Edo** ●江戸	Shimosaka school 下坂系 ● Yasutsugu 康継 Tsuguhira 継平 Izumi no Kami Kaneshige 和泉守兼重 Kazusa no Suke Kaneshige 上総介兼重 Yamato no Kami Yasusada 大和守安定 Kotetsu school 虎徹系 ● Kotetsu Okisato 虎徹興里 Okimasa 興正 Okihisa 興久 Hojoji school 法城寺系 ● Masahiro 正弘 Sadakuni 貞国 Kunimitsu 国光 Ishido school 石堂系 ● Korekazu 是一 Mitsuhira 光平 Tsunemitsu 常光 Hankei 繁慶 Hansho 繁昌 Suishinshi school 水心子系 ● Masahide 正秀 Sadahide 貞秀 Naotane 直胤 Naokatsu 直勝 Masayoshi 正義 Masatsugu 正次 Kiyomaro school 清麿系 ● Kiyomaro 清麿 Masao 真雄 Kiyondo 清人 Nobuhide 信秀 Masao 正雄 Chounsai Tsunatoshi 長運斎綱俊 Koyama Munetsugu 固山宗次 Tairyusai Sokan 泰龍斎宗寛 Sa Yukihide 左行秀
	Hitachi ●常陸	Bandotaro Bokuden 坂東太郎卜伝 Ichige Tokurin (Norichika) 市毛徳鄰 Katsumura Tokukatsu 勝村徳勝

● Tokaido 東海道	**Owari** ●尾張	Masatsune school 政常系 ● Sagami no Kami Masatsune 相模守政常 　Mino no Kami Masatsune 美濃守政常 Nobutaka school 信高系 ● Hoki no Kami Nobutaka 伯耆守信高
	Sagami ●相模	Tsunahiro 綱広
● Tosando 東山道	**Rikuzen** ●陸前	Kunikane school 国包系 ● Yamashiro Daijo Kunikane 山城大掾国包 　Yamashiro no Kami Kunikane 山城守国包 Yasutomo school 安倫系 (Yasutomo 安倫)
	Iwashiro ●岩代	Miyoshi school 三善系 ● Aizu Nagakuni 会津長国 Aizu Masanaga 会津政長 　Miyoshi Nagamichi 三善長道
	Mino ●美濃	Shinano no Kami Daido 信濃守大道 Okachiyama Nagasada 御勝山永貞
	Omi ●近江	Sasaki Ippo 佐々木一峯
● Hokurikudo 北陸道	**Kaga** ●加賀	Kanewaka school 兼若系 ● 　Kanewaka 兼若 Takahira 高平 Kagehira 景平 Kiyohira 清平 Kiyomitsu school 清光系 ● Kiyomitsu 清光 Yukimitsu 行光 Darani Katsukuni 陀羅尼勝国
	Echizen ●越前	Shimosaka school 下坂系 ● Yasutsugu 康継 (Edo 江戸) 　Higo Daijo Sadakuni 肥後大掾貞国 Kanenori 兼法 Shigetaka 重高 Masanori 正則 Horikawa school 堀川系 ● Yamashiro no Kami Kunikiyo 山城守国清
● Sanyodo 山陽道	**Harima** ●播磨	Tegarayama Ujishige 手柄山氏繁
	Bizen ●備前	Kozuke Daijo Sukesada 上野大掾祐定 Shichibe no Jo Sukesada 七兵衛尉祐定 Sukenaga 祐永 Sukekane 祐包
	Bitchu ●備中	Mizuta Kunishige 水田国重
	Aki ●安芸	Higo no Kami Teruhiro 肥後守輝広 Harima no Kami Teruhiro 播磨守輝広

Nankaido ● 南海道	**Kii** ●紀伊	Nanki Shigekuni 南紀重国 Monju Shigekuni 文珠重国
	Tosa ●土佐	Sa Yukihide 左行秀 (Edo 江戸) Nankai Taro Tomotaka 南海太郎朝尊 (Kyoto 京都)
Saikaido ● 西海道	**Chikuzen** ●筑前	Nobukuni school 信国系 ● 　Yoshikane 吉包 Yoshimasa 吉政 Shigekane 重包 Yoshikane 吉包 Ishido school 石堂系 ● Moritsugu 守次 Koretsugu 是次
	Chikugo ●筑後	Onizuka Yoshikuni 鬼塚吉国
	Bungo ●豊後	Takada school 高田系 ● Fujiwara Yukinaga 藤原行長 Muneyuki 統行 Sadayuki 貞行
	Hizen ●肥前	Iyo no Jo Munetsugu 伊予掾宗次 1st Gen.Tadayoshi 忠吉 2nd Gen. Tadahiro 忠広 3rd Gen.Tadayoshi 忠吉 1st Gen. Masahiro 正広 2nd Gen. Masahiro 正広 1st Gen. Tadakuni 忠国 2nd Gen.Tadakuni 忠国 1st Gen. Yukihiro 行広 2nd Gen. Yukihiro 行広
	Satsuma ●薩摩	Izu no Kami Masafusa 伊豆守正房 Bingo no Kami Ujifusa 備後守氏房 Mondo no Kami Masakiyo 主水正正清 Masamori 正盛 Masachika 正近 Ichinohira Yasuyo 一平安代 Yasuari 安在 Yamato no Kami Motohira 大和守元平 Mototake 元武 Hoki no Kami Masayuki 伯耆守正幸

Date Inscriptions on Swords

Japanese swordsmiths inscribe the tang of their swords with their signature. However, since the early Kamakura period (1185-1333) swords began to also have the date of manufacture inscribed. In addition, since the mid-Kamakura period the use of the sexagenary calendar can be seen to have been used. This system of dating is referred to as Eto, and can be seen to be used in all periods of sword manufacture, as well as on sword fittings of the Edo Period (1603-1868). The practice continues today.

The Ten Stems 十干		The Twelve Animals of the Zodiac 十二支	
Kinoe	甲	*Ne* 子	(Rat 鼠)
Kinoto	乙	*Ushi* 丑	(Ox 牛)
Hinoe	丙	*Tora* 寅	(Tiger 虎)
Hinoto	丁	*U* 卯	(Rabbit 兎)
Tsuchinoe	戊	*Tatsu* 辰	(Dragon 竜)
Tsuchinoto	己	*Mi* 巳	(Snake 蛇)
Kanoe	庚	*Uma* 午	(Horse 馬)
Kanoto	辛	*Hitsuji* 未	(Goat 羊)
Mizunoe	壬	*Saru* 申	(Monkey 猿)
Mizunoto	癸	*Tori* 酉	(Rooster 鶏)
		Inu 戌	(Dog 犬)
		I 亥	(Boar 猪)

The sexagenary calendar in Japan is referred to as Eto. It consists of ten main stems in combination with twelve animals of the zodiac. For example when the first main stem, Kinoe 甲, is combined with the first branch animal, ne 子, it is written Kinoe-ne 甲子. The various combinations create a 60 year cyclical calendar.

Places to See Japanese Swords

The Japanese Sword Museum

The Japanese Sword Museum is a non-profit organization and the home of the Society for the preservation of Japanese Art Swords (NBTHK). The museum opened in 1968. It houses around two-hundred blades, koshirae, fittings, armor, and metal-works. Among those are many National Treasures and Important Cultural Properties.

In addition to regular exhibitions of excellent works, the museum also hosts various exhibitions and is instrumental in the preservation of the traditional skills of the current craftsmen (including swordsmiths, polishers and scabbard makers) by holding an annual competition with an exhibition of the works of the prize winners.

The museum also has a library with approximate 1500 documents dating from the Muromachi period through to the Edo Period. In addition, the museum also holds monthly classes on sword etiquette and appraisal meetings where partcipants can improve their sword knowledge.

The Society for the Preservation of Japanese Art Swords
(Nihon Bijutsu Token Hozon Kyokai: NBTHK)

The society was formed in the turmoil following the Second World War to save Japanese swords from the terrible fate of destruction. Then in 1948, the society was given the approval by the Ministry of Education to introduce the art of Japanese swords to the world.

By 1968, the Japanese Sword Museum was completed, and in 1976, in order to preserve the manufacture of the traditional raw materials for production of Japanese swords, the Nittoho Tatara was opened. Later, the tamahagane production process (Tatara-buki) was recognised as a Important Traditional Craft Designated for Preservation.In addition to managing the Japanese Sword Museum and the Nittoho Tatara, the NBTHK also hold regular appreciation meetings, and provide an appraisal service of Japanese swords, fittings and mountings. They also hold study groups for craftsmen, publish a monthly magazine, and promote sword preservation around the world.

The Japanese Sword Museum

1-12-9 Yokoami
Sumida, Tokyo 130-0015
Tel:+81(0)3 6284 1000   Fax:+81(0)3 6284 1100
http://www.touken.or.jp/museum/
Closed: Mondays

Museums of the World Where You Can See Japanese Swords

OUTSIDE OF JAPAN

The British Museum
Great Russell St
London WC1B 3DG
United Kingdom
Tel: +44 (0)20 7323 8299
http://www.britishmuseum.org

Royal Armouries Museum
Armouries Dr,
Leeds LS10 1LT
United Kingdom
Tel: +44 113 220 1999
http://www.royalarmouries.org

The Tower of London
London EC3N 4AB,
United Kingdom
Tel: +44 (0)20 3166 6000
http://www.hrp.org.uk/tower-of-london/

Chiddingstone Castle
Hill Hoath Road,
Chiddingstone,
Edenbridge,
Kent TN8 7AD,
United Kingdom
Tel: +44 (0)1892 870347
Closed: Thursdays, Fridays and
Saturdays
http://www.chiddingstonecastle.org.uk/

The New York Metropolitan Museum
1000 Fifth Avenue
New York, NY 10028
USA
Tel: +1 212 535 7710
http://www.metmuseum.org

The Museum of Fine Arts, Boston
465 Huntington Ave,
Boston, MA 02115,
USA
Tel: +1 617 267 9300
http://www.mfa.org/

The Stibbert Museum
Via Federigo Stibbert 26,
50134 Firenze,
Italy
Tel: +39 055 486049
Closed: Thursdays
http://www.museostibbert.it/en

Museum Volkenkunde
Steenstraat 1,
2312 BS Leiden,
Netherlands
Tel: +31 88 004 2800
Closed: Mondays
https://volkenkunde.nl/en

JAPAN

Tokyo National Museum

13-9 Ueno Koen,
Taito, Tokyo,
Japan 110-8712
Tel: +81 (0)3 5777 8600
Closed: Mondays
http://www.tnm.jp

Nezu Museum

6-5-1 Minami Aoyama,
Minato, Tokyo
Japan 107-0062
Tel: +81 (0)3 3400 2536
Closed: Mondays
http://www.nezu-muse.or.jp

Seikado Bunko Art Museum

2-23-1 Okamoto,
Setagaya, Tokyo
Japan 157-0076
Tel: +81 (0)3 5405 8686 (English)
Closed: Mondays
http://www.seikado.or.jp/english.html

Eisei Bunko

1-1-1 Mejirodai,
Bunkyo, Tokyo
Japan 112-0015
Tel: +81 (0)3 3941 0850
Closed: Mondays
http://www.eiseibunko.com

Sano Art Museum

1-43 Nakatamachi,
Mishima,
Shizuoka prefecture,
Japan 411-0838
Tel: +81 (0)55 975 7278
Closed: Thursdays
http://www.sanobi.or.jp

Sakakimachi Museum of Tetsu

6313-2 Sakaki,
Sakaki-machi, Hanishinagun,
Nagano prefecture,
Japan 389-0601
Tel: +81 (0)268 82 1128
Closed: Mondays
http://www.tetsu-museum.info

Tokugawa Art Museum

1017 Tokugawa-cho,
Higashi ward, Nagoya,
Aichi prefecture,
Japan 461-0023
Tel: +81 (0)52 935 6262
Closed: Mondays
http://www.tokugawa-art-museum.jp

Bizen Osafune Japanese Sword Museum

966 Osafune,
Osafune-cho,
Setouchi,
Okayama prefecture,
Japan 701-4271
Tel: +81 (0)869 66 7767
Closed: Mondays
http://www.city.setouchi.lg.jp/token/

Glossary

A

Aizame
A type of shark-skin.

Aoi-mon
The triple-hollyhock mon of the Tokugawa clan.

Ashi
(Lit. legs), line extending from the hamon towards the cutting edge.

Ashi-kanamono
Fittings attached to the saya that attach to the obi-tori.

Ayasugi-hada
Undulating grain pattern in the ji resembling a Japanese cedar grain pattern.

B

Bakumatsu
An era in the late Edo period 1853-1867.

Bizen
Archeaic province of Japan, modern day Okayama prefecture.

Bo-hi
Long groove, carved into the blade, often mistakenly referred to as a blood groove.

Bonji
Sanscrit characters carved into the blade invoking Buddhist deities.

Boshi
Literally 'cap', the hamon formed within the kissaki.

C

Chikei
A curved line of nie, seen in the ji.

Choji midare
A hamon consisting of choji shapes, but the overall line of the hamon has no definable form.

Choji oil
Clove oil, used for preserving blades.

Chokuto
A straight sword, but similar in construction to the tachi.

Chu-kissaki
A medium sized kissaki, in relation to the overall size of the blade.

Chumon-uchi
Specially ordered blades.

Chu-suguha
A medium-sized straight hamon.

D

Daimyo
Provincial samurai lords.

Daisho
A pair of swords in matching fittings worn together: dai-being the long sword, and sho-being the shorter companion sword. Only the samurai were permitted to wear them during the Edo period.

Denchu-kojiri
This type of kojiri is wider than the koi-guchi, and is angular with one side longer than the other.

Den
A lineage, or style.

E

Edo period
1600-1868.

Eto
Zodiacal calender often used for date inscriptions on swords, originally from China.

F

Fuchi
A decorative reinforcing collar attached to the base of the tsuka.

Fuchi-kanamono
See fuchi.

Fudo Myo-o
A Buddhist deity with an angry expression commonly used for horimono. An incarnation of the Dainichi Buddha.

Fukurin
A gold, silver, or bronze band attached to the tsuba.

Funbari
Used to describe a blade when it noticeably widens at the base of the cutting edge.

Futasuji-hi
Two parallel grooves carved into the blade.

G

Gendaito
Japanese swords produced after 1912.

Gokaden
The five original traditions of swordmaking from the Koto period.

Goki-shichido
The five home provinces and seven main roads. Originally used for units of governmental administration. Currently used for classifying swordsmiths by region and style.

Gomabashi
A type of horimono of parallel grooves that represent the hibashi (metal chopsticks) used for a ceremony that invokes the deity Fudo Myo-o.

Gunome
A type of hamon that undulates in a series of semi-circles.

Gunto
Military blades.

H

Ha
The hardened part of the blade along the cutting edge.

Habaki
The small metal collar (often decorated) that buffers the tsuba and secures the blade into the saya.

Habaki-moto
The part of the blade that sits under the habaki.

Hachiman-daibosatsu
A diety often revered by warriors.

Hada
The pattern on the steel skin of the blade, also called jihada.

Hadori
A polishing technique which highlights the hamon, also known as kesho.

Haitorei
The law administered in Japan 1876, banning the wearing of swords in public.

Hakikake
Similar to sunagashi, resembling brush strokes in the boshi.

Ha-machi
The notch where the cutting edge of the blade begins.

Hamon
The crystalline structure which forms along the cutting edge of a blade as a result of the hardening process.

Hataraki
The various activities within the hamon, created during the hardening process.

Heian Period
794-1185.

Hi
A groove carved into the blade for weight decreasing or decoration purposes.

Hira-zukuri
A sword made without any ridgelines, flat on both sides.

Hiro-suguha
A wide suguha hamon.

Hiru-maki
A flat type of wrap.

Hitatsura
A hamon with lots of tobiyaki, so that most of the blade os hardened.

Horimono
Decorative blade carvings.

Hyogo-gusari Koshirae
A very durable and practical type of tachi koshirae that was popular with high-ranking samurai warriors of the late 12th Century. Hyogo-gusari koshirae ashi are constructed from chain.

I

Ichimai-boshi
A type of boshi that covers, or almost covers the entire kissaki.

Ichimonji school
A 13th C school of swordsmiths working in the Bizen tradition.

Ichi-no-ashi
The ashi-kanamono closest to the saya mouth.

Ie-bori
Fittings makers in the employ of the Bakufu. Namely the Goto family.

Ikakeji
A type of lacquer with very fine gold flakes.

Ikubi kissaki
A stout kissaki which is shorter in length than it is wide.

Iori-mune
A two-sided mune resembling the roof of a house.

Ishizuki
The scabbard chape attached to protect the saya-jiri.

Itame-hada
A type of wood grain pattern in the skin steel of the blade.

Ito-maki-tachi Koshirae
A type of tachi koshirae that has the wrapping on the handle repeated on the upper part of the saya.

J

Ji
The surface area of the blade between the shinogi and the hamon.

Jigane
The steel of a constructed blade.

Jihada
The surface area of the blade between the hamon and the shinogi, see hada.

Ji-nie
Nie in the ji.

K

Kabuto-gane
A pommel cap for the tsuka.

Kaeri
The part of the boshi that turns back towards the tang, along the mune.

Kaeri-zuno
A small hook on the saya to stop the saya coming out of the belt.

Kaiken
A small concealable dagger.

Kamakura period
1185-1333.

Kanbun Shinto
Blades made around the Kanbun era 1661-1673.

Kara tsuba
A Chinese style tsuba.

Kasane
The thickness of the blade.

Kashira
A decorative pommel attached to reinforce the end of the tsuka.

Katana
Curved blades worn with the cutting edge up, when thrust through the sash.

Katte-agari yasuri
Filemarks on the tang that slant downward to the left.

Katte-sagari yasuri
Filemarks on the tang that slant downward to the right.

Kazari-tachi Koshirae
Richly decorated formal tachi koshirae that were popular during the peak of the aristocratic government in the Nara and Heian periods.

Kazari-byo
See Tawara-byo.

Kazu-uchi mono
Mass produced blades of little artistic quality.

Ken
Straight ritual Chinese style sword, often associated with Fudo Myo-o.

Keicho era
1596-1615.

Keicho Shinto
Blades produced around the Keicho era (1596-1614) at the start of the Shinto sword period.

Kesho
See Hadori.

Kin-Nashiji
A gold colored lacquered ground that resembles Japanese pear skin.

Kinsuji
A small shiny line of nie inside the hamon, similar to inazuma.

Kinzogan-mei
A gold inlaid inscription.

Kiriha-zukuri
A sword made with the shinogi close to the cutting edge.

Kirikomi
Cut marks in a sword made by another sword.

Kiri yasuri
Filemarks on the tang that are horizontal.

Kissaki
The tip of the blade, from the point to the yokote.

Ko
Prefix, meaning small (ex. Ko-nie—small nie).

Ko-Bizen
The old Bizen school of swordsmiths.

Kobuse
The most common type of blade manufacture, in which the steel used for the cutting edge is wrapped around a lower carbon steel, then hammered out into the shape of the blade.

Kogai
A bodkin like implement with a small scoop on the end used for fixing a samurai's hair and cleaning his ears.

Kogatana
Utility knife.

Koi-guchi
The mouth of the saya.

Ko-itame
Small wood grain pattern.

Kojiri
A decorative fitting on the bottom of the saya.

Ko-maru
A type of boshi that turns back in a small smooth circular motion.

Ko-midare
An almost straight kind of hamon with small undulations.

Ko-nie
Small nie particles.

Koshirae
A full set of sword mountings.

Koshi-zori
A blade with the center of curvature in the base or handle.

Koto
(Old swords) Swords made prior the Edo period.

Kozuka
A term used to refer to both a decorative handle for a small utility knife and for the complete handle and knife assembled together.

Kuchi-kanamono
A metal fitting at the koi-guchi.

Kuichigai-ba
A break in the hamon, common in yamato-den blades.

Kuri-jiri
Round-ended type of nakago, similar to the shape of a chestnut.

Kurikara
A horimono of a dragon wrapped around a ken, a representation of Fudo Myo-o.

Kurigata
A nodule with a hole affixed on the outside of the saya to attach the sageo.

Kuyo-mon
The crest of the Hosokawa family.

M

Machi
The notches that mark the end of the mune; mune-machi and the end of the cutting edge; ha-machi.

Machi-bori
Fittings makers not in the direct employ of the Bakufu.

Maru-mune
A mune that is rounded.

Masame-hada
A straight grain pattern in the hada.

Masamune
(Circa .13-14th C.), widely recognized as Japan's greatest swordsmith.

Mei
Signature or inscription on the tang.

Mekugi
The bamboo peg used to secure the handle onto the tang.

Mekugi ana
The hole on the tang where the mekugi is inserted.

Mekugi nuki
A tool for removing the mekugi.

Menuki
Decorative hand grips affixed to both sides of the tsuka.

Midare komi
A boshi where the a midare hamon continues into the kissaki.

Midare
A hamon of irregular form. All hamon are midare except suguha.

Mi-haba
The width of a blade: measured from the mune to the cutting edge.

Mitsu-mune
A mune with three sides.

Mokume-hada
A grain pattern in the hada similar to itame but round.

Monouchi
One-third of the blade from the yokote towards the tang.

Moto-haba
The width of the blade at the base.

Mune
The back of the blade.

Mune-machi
See machi.

N

Naga-kazari
Long fittings on kazari-tachi koshirae.

Nagasa
The blade length; measured from the tip to the mune-machi.

Naginata
A Japanese halberd.

Nakago
The tang of a blade.

Nakago-jiri
The tip of the tang.

Nanatsu-gane
Metal fittings used for adjusting the length of the obi-tori. There are three on the ichi-no-ashi, and four on the ni-no-ashi.

Nanbokucho Period
1333-1392.

Nashiji
Pear skin ground.

Nie
Small martensite crystals individually visible to the naked eye.

Nie-deki
A blade with a predominantly nie hamon.

Nihon Bijutsu Token Hozon Kyokai
The Society for the Preservation of Japanese art Swords: The Japanese Sword Museum in Tokyo.

Nihonto
Japanese swords.

Niju-ba
Lines of nie or nioi running parallel to the hamon.

Ni-no-ashi

The ashi-kanamono furthest away from the saya mouth.

Nioi

Martensite crystals not individually distinguishable to the naked eye. Similar to the mistiness of the milky way in appearance.

Nioi-deki

A sword with a hamon consisting mainly of nioi.

No-dachi

Long swords popular during the Nanbokucho period.

Notare

Gently undulating hamon.

O

O

Prefix, denoting large (ex. O-gunome—large gunome).

Obi-tori

Suspension straps for a belt is passed through for a tachi to be worn in a slung fashion.

O-dachi

A tachi with a cutting edge that exceeds 3 shaku (91cm).

O-hada

Large hada pattern.

O-kissaki

A large sized kissaki.

O-maru

A type of boshi that turns back in a large smooth circular motion.

O-seppa

Large sized spacers (seppa) that match the shape of the tsuba.

Osafune

A prolific swordsmithing village in Bizen province.

R

Raden

Mother of Pearl.

S

Sageo

A cord attached to the kurigata to help secure the sword in the belt.

Saka-ashi

Slanted ashi.

Saki-haba

Width of the blade at the yokote.

Saki-togaru

A type of boshi where the tip is pointed.

Saki-zori

When the curvature is noticeable in the upper part of the blade.

Sanjuban-shin

A group of thirty deities.

Sanko-tsuki-ken

A double edged straight sword with a three pronged hilt.

Sarute

A ring for the attachment of a te-nukio.

Saya

Scabbard.

Saya-guchi

See Koi-guchi.

Saya-jiri

The bottom of the outside of the saya.

Semegane

A decorated metal band that supports the saya between the ni-no-ashi and the ishizuke.

Sengoku period

Age of the warring states 1493-1573.

Seppa

Spacers that fit between the tsuka and the tsuba, and between the tsuba and the habaki to ensure the tsuka fits perfectly.

Shaku

Japanese imperial form of measurement (1 shaku = 30.3cm).

Shinogi

The ridgeline that that runs from the yokote to the end of the nakago.

Shinogi-ji
The area between the shinogi and the mune.

Shinogi-zukuri
A sword manufactured with the ridgeline near to the mune.

Shin-shinto
(New, new swords) Swords made between 1764 and 1876.

Shinto
(New swords) Swords made between 1600 and 1764.

Shirasaya
A plain wooden sleeping scabbard and handle to protect the blade.

Shitodome
Decorative metal flanges used on the kurikata and the kashira.

Shogun
The title of the military leader of Japan between 1192 to 1867.

Sori
Curvature of the blade.

Soshu-den
The tradition of swordmaking originating from the archaic Sagami province.

Suguha
A straight hamon.

Sujikai yasuri
Acutely slanted filemark pattern on the nakago.

Sukashi
Openwork. i.e. Sukashi-tsuba.

Su-ken
Also known as a ken, short straight ritual Chinese style sword, often associated with Fudo Myo-O.

Sun
Japanese imperial form of measurement (1 sun = 3.03cm, 10 sun = 1 shaku).

Sunagashi
An activity in the hamon that resembles sweeping sands.

Suriage
Blade that has been shortened from its original length.

T

Tachi
Swords made to be worn with the cutting edge down, suspended from the belt.

Taiko-gane
A decorated metal stud used to fix the ashi-kawa. Often in the design of a clan mon.

Tamahagane
Indigenous Japanese steel, used for the manufacture of Japanese swords.

Tanto
Blades with a cutting edge shorter that 30cm.

Tawara-byo
Decorative pins originally used to secure the same-gawa on old tachi.

Togari-ba
Pointed shapes protruding from the hamon.

Toran-ba
A type of hamon that resembles the waves of the sea.

Tsuba
A Japanese sword guard.

Tsuchioki
The clay applied to the blade before the hardening process.

Tsuka
The hilt.

Tsuka-maki
The wrap on a tsuka (hilt).

Tsukuri-komi
Blade construction.

U

Ubu
Original, commonly used when referring to the nakago.

Uchi-gatana
Blades produced for one-handed use during the Muromachi period worn thrust through the belt with the cutting edge uppermost.

Uchi-gatana Koshirae

A general term for practical sword mountings of the Sengoku period. Also known as katana-koshirae.

Uchi-gumori

One of the last stones used in the foundation polishing process.

Uchiko

A fine powder, made from one of the stones used in sword polishing, used for sword preservation.

Uchinoke

Small crescent shapes appearing like niju-ba in the ji close to the hamon.

Uchi-zori

The back of the blade curves toward the cutting edge.

Urushi

Japanese lacquer.

Utsuri

(Reflection) A white misty formation that runs parallel to the hamon in the ji.

Utsushi-mono

Copies of past masterpieces (not to be confused with forgeries).

Wakizashi

Blades with a cutting edge of over 30 cm in length, but shorter than 60 cm. Often a companion sword to the katana.

Watari-maki

The wrapping that matches the tsuka-maki on an ito-maki-tachi that runs from the koi-guchi to just past the ni-no-ashi.

Watetsu

Japanese steel.

Yagura-gane

A ring type fitting that allows the obi-tori to be attached to the yamagata-kanamono.

Yaki-ire

The hardening process of the blade when it is heated, then quenched in water.

Yakizume

A type of boshi without a turn-back.

Yari

A Japanese spear usually mounted on a long shaft.

Yamagata-kanamono

The mountain shaped parts of the ashi-kanamono.

Yamato

Archeaic province of Japan, modern day Nara prefecture.

Yasurime

File markings (on the tang).

Yo

An activity in the hamon that resembles falling leaves.

Yokote-suji

The dividing line between the kissaki and the body of the blade (mainly on shinogi-zukuri swords).

Cooperation ● The Japanese Sword Museum Curatorial Section,
All Japan Swordsmiths Association, TV-Setouchi Create Co., Ltd,
Japanese Sword Research Foundation Kiyoshi Sawaguchi (PhD),
Mari Sekihashi (office Kai)

Art direction & Design ● Takashi Hasebe (hasebe design office)
Design ● Ikuno Negishi (hasebe design office)
Illustration ● Mizuta Design (Sumio Mizuta, Takahiro Muneoka): p.24 (haniwa), p.27 (person),
p.29 (person), p.39 (person), p.46 (person), p.52, 55, 56, 59, 60, 62, 68-81, 84-91, 99, 101
Yuki Imoto: p.38-45   Yuki Yoshimura: others
Photo ● Ryo Kubo

A Beginner's Illustrated Handbook

Swords of Japan

2016年9月15日　初版第1刷発行
2019年6月15日　初版第4刷発行

著　　者　　久保恭子
翻　　訳　　ポール・マーティン
発 行 者　　鎌田章裕
発 行 所　　株式会社東京美術
　　　　　　〒170-0011　東京都豊島区池袋本町3-31-15
　　　　　　電話　03 (5391) 9031
　　　　　　FAX　03 (3982) 3295
　　　　　　http://www.tokyo-bijutsu.co.jp
印刷・製本　　大日本印刷株式会社

ISBN978-4-8087-1071-2 C0072
©TOKYO BIJUTSU Co., Ltd. 2016　Printed in Japan